A FIELD GUIDE TO DIPSH*TS

The Ultimate Survival Manual

Also by Dale Hartley:

Machiavellians: Gulling the Rubes
GullingTheRubes.com

A FIELD GUIDE TO DIPSH*TS

The Ultimate Survival Manual

Dale Hartley, PhD

Ockham Publishing

Published in 2023 by Ockham Publishing in the United Kingdom

ISBN: 978-1-83919-553-2

www.ockham-publishing.com

Contents

Preface

Stultus est sicut stultus facit[1]

Why would a brilliant neurosurgeon drive 138 miles per hour on a city street where the posted speed limit is 45, ultimately crashing and killing his passenger?

What prompts a convicted felon, who cannot legally possess a firearm, to carry one through airport security and then to fire the weapon when he's caught?

How could a biology professor continue importing endangered wildlife specimens without declaring them after being warned three times by customs officials?

What exactly is a dipsh*t? You may have your own definition, or maybe you just "know one when you see one." Our lives are beset by these remarkably reckless and irresponsible individuals. They create havoc and leave chaos in their wake. Most of us need look no further than our extended family, neighborhood, workplace, or the daily headlines to find plenty of examples. Even when we can recognize them on sight, that may not be enough to protect us from getting caught in the fallout from their misdeeds. We need a way to size them up and deal with them proactively. This book will show you how to do precisely that.

---

[1] "Stupid is as stupid does."

In chapter one I provide an exact definition of "dipsh*t" that guides the narrative throughout the succeeding chapters. Only when we acknowledge that these noxious nincompoops are a fact of life and that they pose a real threat can we take steps to guard against them. I call this book a "field guide" and "survival manual" to emphasize that you will encounter dipsh*ts in daily life, that they come in several different varieties, and that you should know how to classify and cope with them when their misconduct affects you. In short, forewarned is forearmed.

Throughout this book you'll find examples of both smart and not-too-bright people acting with reckless abandon. Intelligence, education, wealth, social status, gender, age, race, religion, and nationality are irrelevant. Being human is all that's required. And while the United States seems to produce an overabundance of these nitwits, you'll find examples in these pages from many nations and all walks of life.

When irritated by just the right provocations, even the most sanguine and peace-loving among us can turn to dipsh*ttery. You'll read about a situation when I lapsed into that kind of behavior myself. I'd like to think that most of us strive to conduct ourselves decently even when we're tempted to "release the Kraken." But there are some people who seem to embrace the dipsh*t lifestyle. Many such cases feature in the following chapters. Some of their stories are funny, some are shocking, and some are outrageous.

I'll introduce you to the *Ten Laws of Dipsh*ttery* beginning in the first chapter, after which I'll devote an entire chapter to discussing each of these laws. Every chapter begins with a remarkable true story that illustrates the current theme, followed by additional examples dispersed throughout the chapter. After presenting these cases, I advance several theories that shed light on the boneheaded behavior in those factual accounts. By the time you finish this book, dipsh*ts should no longer be a "riddle wrapped in a mystery inside an enigma" (as Churchill said of Russia).

In these pages you'll also encounter *dipsh*t analytics* for the first time. It's a handy method for assessing and ranking them based on four categorical factors. This quick and easy technique can be your superpower against them.

"Dipsh*t," of course, is not a diagnostic term, nor does it specify a personality disorder. It indicates someone who engages in a disruptive or destructive pattern of behavior which can be recognized based on the criteria presented in chapter one. Some people who behave reprehensibly or recklessly do have one or more personality disorders. But then again, each of us can act irresponsibly at times. A personality disorder may be a contributing factor in some cases, but a clinical condition is certainly not a prerequisite for dipsh*ttery.

Even though this book isn't about applying a diagnosis, it is about abnormal psychology. Dipsh*t behavior is not normal. Someone who occasionally acts foolishly is not necessarily an abnormal person, even though his or her behavior at that moment may be so. We'd all be abnormal if an isolated instance of irresponsibility could brand us with that label. The word "abnormal" would then lack any relevance. In the context of psychology, "abnormal" means extreme behaviors, whether acute or chronic, that create reasonable doubt about a person's mental state and competence. Frequency, type and degree of abnormality, context, and the extent to which others are adversely affected must be taken into consideration.

Please note that we should not label children, non-adult teenagers, and profoundly mentally ill individuals as dipsh*ts, no matter how noxious their behavior might be. That would be unfair, unethical, and cruel. People who are incapable of exercising mature judgment or of foreseeing the consequences of their behavior, shouldn't be blamed or mocked. Let's reserve the "d-word" for adults who not only deserve it, but who by their cretinous conduct are practically begging for it.

Unfortunately, we can't always steer clear of dipsh*ts or disentangle ourselves from them before we've become their victims. This book recommends specific tactics you can use whenever you find yourself ensnared (or about to be) by their recklessness or negligence. One tactic I don't recommend, however, is confrontation. No matter how tempting it may be to directly challenge dipsh*ttery, you'll usually find that such an approach only makes matters worse. But you'll read more about that in the chapters dealing with the Ten Laws.

Finally, I close with this admonishment (and I include myself among those who need to heed it): Let us conduct ourselves so that our lives serve as an example to others, and not as a warning. As for the latter, the dipsh*ts already have that covered.

* * *

"There is nothing more frightening than ignorance in action."
– Johann Wolfgang von Goethe

Chapter One

The Quintessence of the Dipsh*t

It was four days before Thanksgiving in 2021. Picture the lines and borderline chaos at security checkpoints in the Atlanta airport. A Transportation Security Administration (TSA) officer monitoring the baggage scanner noticed something suspicious in a piece of luggage and flagged it for manual inspection. The bag and its owner were taken aside.

As he opened the questionable carry-on, the inspecting officer directed the passenger, 42-year-old Kenny Wells, not to touch or reach into the bag. Suddenly, Wells did just that. He lunged for the pistol he had been trying to smuggle through security. The gun accidentally discharged, creating a stampede of frightened passengers. Wells fled the scene with his weapon.

Luckily, no one was wounded when Wells' weapon fired, but a few people were injured during the ensuing melee. Two travelers had to be evacuated to a hospital. All checkpoints were shut down temporarily. The airport grounded all flights pending an "all clear" announcement from TSA.

Wells' attempt to board a flight with a loaded gun cascaded throughout the Atlanta airport and beyond. When TSA shut down the checkpoints, many passengers missed their flights and had to rebook during one of the busiest travel weeks of the year.

People who had already boarded their flights found themselves confined aboard aircraft that couldn't move. When flights finally received clearance for takeoff, they were so delayed that passengers missed their connections. The rebooking of passengers aboard late flights had to be repeated at several other airports. Many people experienced fear, frustration, expense, and interrupted Thanksgiving plans because of one irredeemable dipsh*t.

Police issued a warrant for Wells' arrest, and he turned himself in about a week later. As a convicted felon with a long rap sheet, Wells could not legally possess a gun. At his preliminary hearing, the judge denied bond. Facing multiple charges, Wells agreed to plead guilty to one count of felonious possession of a firearm. The prosecution and defense jointly agreed to recommend a sentence of 10 years.

The Transportation Security Administration confiscated 6.542 guns from airline passengers in 2022 – more than any previous year and a 10% increase over 2021. Many of the firearms, 88% of them loaded, were seized from cretins like Kenny Wells who tried to take them through security checkpoints. Some guns were seized from non-secure checked luggage. (Firearms can be transported in checked baggage, but they must be unloaded, declared to the airline, and secured in a locked, hard-sided case.)

In the post-9/11 era, how can anyone not know that attempting to board a commercial flight with a firearm is a serious offense? Until recently travelers couldn't even take nail clippers onto a plane. A typical excuse from gun-toting scofflaws is that they "forgot" about the gun in their bag. That excuse goes over about as well with TSA as "the dog ate my homework" went over in tenth grade. It's a gun. If you're the type that feels compelled to stash a concealed weapon in a suitcase, then you're expected to know where it is at all times. No excuses.

By the way, fines for getting caught with a gun at a U.S. airport range from $3,000 to $14,950.

Wherefore, Dipsh*t?

If we're going to call anyone a dipsh*t, it might as well be Kenny Wells (bless his heart).

WSB-TV reported that his rap sheet "between 1997 and 2015 [included] burglary, forgery, impersonating an officer, false imprisonment, theft by taking, and possession of a firearm by a convicted felon." He knew that he wasn't allowed to have a gun. He also knew that the weapon could get him sent back to prison on a parole violation. Yet he procured a pistol, took it with him (loaded) to the airport, tried to smuggle it past an x-ray scanner, lunged for it after the TSA officer warned him not to, and accidentally discharged it in his bungling attempt to flee the scene. The magnitude of his senseless misconduct on airports, airlines, and passengers during peak travel season illustrates the destructive potential of reckless and irresponsible people.

The Wells case manifests layer upon layer of breathtakingly boneheaded behavior, each act escalating into another and then another. This raises certain questions: *Who qualifies as a dipsh*t? Where do we draw the line, dipsh*t-wise? What are the essential dipsh*t characteristics? What, if anything, can be done about them?* This book will answer those questions.

Dictionary.com defines "dipsh*t" as "a stupid or despicable person." I have a bone to pick with that definition. "Stupid" I agree with. Likewise, I'm in accord with "despicable." It's the "or" part that misses the mark in my opinion.

You be the judge: Does Kenny Wells' behavior strike you as merely stupid, but not despicable? Or vice versa? At worst we might call a stupid person a dumbass. For a despicable person we might up the ante to asshole or douchebag. But when we say "dipsh*t," we mean someone whose behavior is both dumb and contemptible. Therefore, as used in this book, "dipsh*t" means those calamitous cretins who engage in conduct that's both stupid *and* despicable.

One ethical caveat: It is cruel and unfair to brand children or people with diminished mental capacity as dipsh*ts. The human brain continues to develop until about age 25. I think we should cut adolescents and pre-teens some slack. Remember the foolish and irresponsible things you did during your formative years? Also, by "diminished mental capacity," I mean people who are mentally disabled and profoundly lacking in cognitive abilities. Just having emotional problems or a personality disorder does not excuse negligence, recklessness, or gross incompetence. We all have "issues," but must still act responsibly and with what the law calls "reasonable care."

I, Dipsh*t

While working at my first job after college, one of my female coworkers made my heart go pitter-pat. I invited her to attend an

Elton John concert with me, and she said yes. Little did either of us realize it was to be a date from hell.

The concert took place at a coliseum surrounded by a vast parking lot. We arrived early, found a decent parking spot, and made our way to the nearest entrance. Our seats, as it turned out, gave us an excellent view of the stage.

It would take some serious effort not to enjoy Elton in concert. We were both having a great time. But alas, nature abhors a dipsh*t. Neither I nor my date was to go unpunished.

During the encore, we decided to leave a few minutes early to get ahead of the traffic. I escorted her through a nearby exit, and we headed for my car. When we got to the row where I thought I'd parked, my vehicle wasn't there. We checked up and down adjacent rows, but still didn't find it. That's when I noticed that all the coliseum's entrances looked alike.

The gates were numbered, and that was the only way to tell them apart. I didn't pay attention to the gate number when we entered. And now it was dawning on me that we must have exited through the wrong gate. For all I knew, my car might be parked just a few rows away, or it could be on the other side of the arena.

By this time, the concert crowd had begun to filter out and drive away. It was nearly midnight, and within a few minutes we found ourselves alone and stranded in a vast and creepy concrete desert. This was in the days before cell phones, and there was no pay phone in sight.

And so we wandered the parking lot, lost and bewildered. My date kept her composure, but I'm sure she was vacillating between rage at me and concern for her own safety. Providence, however, sometimes smiles even upon dipsh*ts. After another fifteen minutes or so of fruitless searching, a coliseum security vehicle spotted us. They gave us a ride and helped us locate my car about a quarter of a mile away. There wasn't much conversation as I drove the young lady home.

Needless to say, there were to be no more dates with that coworker. One day about three weeks later, she didn't show up for work. The rumor began to spread that she'd called in and quit abruptly. I can't help but wonder if her sudden departure was motivated by the desire to avoid further contact with a certain dipsh*t.

Toward a Taxonomy of Dipsh*ts

What the world needs, along with peace, love, and free beer in every employee break room, is a convenient rubric for identifying the various types of dipsh*ts and estimating their disruptive potential. This chapter introduces *dipsh*t analytics*, a set of guidelines that will allow you to do just that. We'll begin by sorting dipsh*ts by type.

The Occasional Type

Believe it or not, I'm not a total screw-up. I'm a retired college professor with postgraduate degrees. I've published two books. Before my career in academia, I founded a company that expanded to 14 states and Puerto Rico and lasted for 23 years (the Great Recession of 2008 killed it). So how can a reasonably intelligent and competent person like me also be the kind of schmuck who gets lost in a stadium parking lot? (With remarkable ease, apparently.)

I had to reach all the way back to my post-college years to find a stellar example of my own dipsh*ttery. Since then, I've made my share of mistakes and faux pas, but nothing as humiliating (for me), and vexatious (for my date) as that experience. When I hustled us through the wrong gate and into the erroneous parking area, I was an *occasional* dipsh*t.

Stupefying behavior that's temporary and out of character for a person usually occurs because circumstances somehow contributed to the snafu. I didn't notice our gate number at the coliseum because I was busy talking to my date. My excitement about the concert and the crowd's jostling at the entrance gate also factored into my negligence. These are not good excuses, and I should have paid attention. But I let myself be distracted. My dipsh*ttery was an isolated occurrence.

These are the criteria for identifying the occasional type. All four must be met:

- *Limited* – behavior is confined to a specific time or circumstance.
- *Anomalous* – out of character; person does not have a reputation as a dipsh*t.
- *Triggered* – likely a reaction to a situation, an event, or even a particular person.
- *Consequential* – causes harm to self and/or others ("harm" means anything from being a nuisance to causing catastrophic damage).

The Chronic Type

We don't know Kenny Wells' life story – the hardships he may have endured and the challenges that may have sent him down the wrong path in life. By the time Wells fired off a shot in the Atlanta airport, his record as felon and recidivist qualified him as a *chronic* dipsh*t, regardless of any extenuating circumstances. His airport crime was so senseless and repugnant that it diverts our empathy from Wells to his victims.

Here's another example of the chronic type. Matthew Jason Beddingfield, 22, pleaded guilty to assaulting police officers with a metal flagpole during the January 6, 2021 attack on the U.S. Capitol. (An American flag was still attached to the pole.) He also allegedly hurled a metal rod at police. Beddingfield stormed into the Capitol near the head of the mob, eventually entering Rep. Kevin McCarthy's office. At the time of this offense, Beddingfield was out on bail for an attempted murder charge. Under his plea agreement, he faces a maximum term of eight years.

As is typical, we do not have Beddingfield's life history. But according to the Justice Department he assaulted police, ran amok in the Capitol, conspired to disrupt certification of a presidential election, and breached a congressman's office. That he did this while out on bail for allegedly attempting murder demonstrates a history of mayhem that cannot be dismissed as merely occasional. These facts suggest that he can't or won't govern his aggressive impulses or weigh the potential consequences of his antisocial behavior. Beddingfield qualifies as a chronic type.

Chronic dipsh*t criteria include the following, all of which must be met:

- *Continuous* – behavior is repetitive and impacts many areas of life.
- *Consistent* – the person has a history and reputation as a dipsh*t.
- *Triggered/Untriggered* – behavior may be a reaction to a situation/person/event or may be unprovoked and self-induced.
- *Consequential* – causes harm to self and/or others ("harm" means anything from being a nuisance to causing catastrophic damage).

The Hybrid Type

Richard T. Kazmaier, a former associate professor of biology at West Texas A&M University, received a six-month prison sentence and $5000 fine for violating the Lacey Act, which criminalizes wildlife trafficking. Kazmaier "admitted he imported wildlife items from Bulgaria, Canada, China, the Czech Republic, Indonesia, Latvia, Norway, Russia, South Africa, Spain, the United Kingdom, and Uruguay into Texas without declaring them," the Justice Department said. These were not living creatures but rather "skulls, skeletons, and taxidermy mounts."

According to prosecutors, Kazmaier illegally imported 358 animal artifacts. He faced a possible sentence of 20 years and a $250,000 fine. On at least three occasions, customs inspectors intercepted wildlife shipments addressed to Kazmaier and allowed him to file paperwork retroactively. These three "wake-up calls" were not sufficient to deter his prolific violations.

Kazmaier qualifies as a hybrid type. He engaged in illegal and self-defeating behavior repeatedly and over a prolonged period of time as a chronic dipsh*t would do. But there are mitigating factors. Kazmaier earned at least two graduate degrees including a doctorate in zoology. He performed successfully as an academic, having served first as an assistant professor and then an associate professor from 2001 until 2022. Except for his import violations, he did not have a history of incompetence or recklessness.

Kazmaier confined his problematic behavior to one specific area of his life. In his profession he demonstrated stability and achievement. This is the distinguishing characteristic of hybrid dipsh*ts. They commit obtuse and offensive acts continuously like the chronic type, but in only one aspect of their lives (i.e., limited), like the occasional type.

To qualify as a hybrid dipsh*t, all of the following criteria must be met:

- **Semi-Continuous** – behavior is ongoing but affects only one area of life.
- **Anomalous** – out of character except in one area of life.
- **Untriggered** – behavior is usually self-induced but may be secondarily influenced by situation/person/event.
- **Consequential** – causes harm to self and/or others ("harm" means anything from being a nuisance to causing catastrophic damage).

All three types of these obtuse and offensive individuals can produce the kind of "everybody loses" outcome that Kenny Wells unleashed at the Atlanta airport. Neither stupidity nor despicability alone can explain this. People can be both stupid and innocent, thereby lacking malicious intent. Despicable people can be intelligent and competent (e.g., Vladimir Putin and Kim Jong Un), and therefore not stupid. It takes stupidity and despicability working together to produce the quintessence of dipsh*ttery.

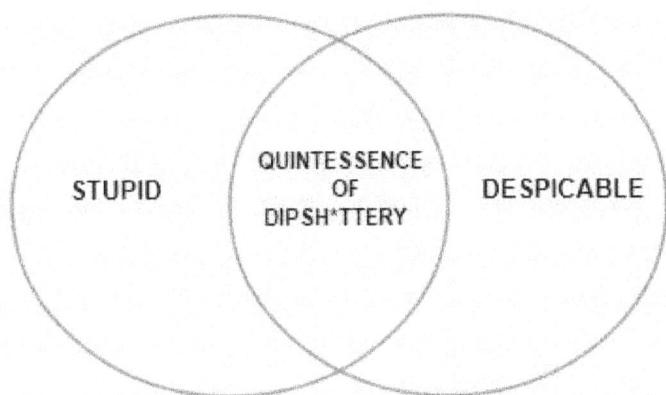

Now that you can classify dipsh*ts as fitting the occasional, chronic, or hybrid patterns, we can proceed to a more thorough analysis of these vexatious pests. In addition to their individual characteristics, it's important to examine the *situation, cause,* and *outcome* of their malfeasance.

Situation

"Situation" refers to the circumstances prevailing at the time of the offensive acts. Situations can be classified as *benign,* such as shopping at a supermarket or walking down a neighborhood street; *frenetic*, such as driving in rush hour traffic or going through airport security; or *provocative*, such as arguing with a store manager about a declined refund or being jostled about in a boisterous crowd. During my fateful date at the concert, I became distracted by conversation, by the crowd, and by my preoccupation with the concert experience. This was a frenetic situation. Knowing this provides context to my behavior but does not excuse it.

Cause

Determining "cause" requires deciding whether a dipsh*t's behavior is *habitual, triggered,* or *self-induced.* Consider Kenny Wells' behavior at the airport. Wasn't he triggered by TSA's search of his bags? At first blush it may seem that way, but given his history I would rate his behavior as habitual. Discovery of the gun was an inevitable consequence of his bringing it to the airport. Certainly, he panicked when he realized he was in trouble. But his habitual irresponsibility and recklessness caused the chain reaction of events that precipitated the airport crisis.

Hillary Mueller, a St. Louis woman, provides an example of someone whose behavior was triggered. Mueller, who is white, observed D'Arreion Toles, a young black man, attempting to enter the condominium complex where she lived. She blocked his path and questioned him about his reason for entering the building.

When Toles declined to explain himself, Mueller refused to move out of his way and demanded that he produce proof of residency. The man recorded a video of the encounter on his phone.

He was in fact a resident of that building. After he finally showed her his key, she let him enter. A short while later, a police officer knocked on his door and told him that Mueller had complained that he made her "uncomfortable." The video went viral, and Mueller (who ironically worked for a minority-owned firm) was fired.

Seeing an unknown black man trying to enter the building apparently triggered Mueller's vigilantism. Presumably she did not waylay and interrogate every male of every race, so why single out this man? It seems obvious what her trigger was.

My concert date devolved into disaster because I didn't pay attention to where I parked or which gate was ours. This was a self-induced situation. Yes, there were distractions, but other people attending the concert managed to remember how they entered and where they parked. The fault was entirely mine.

Outcome

The fallout from stupid and pernicious behavior can be rated according to severity. I recommend a scale of zero to five: 0 (null; negligible effects), 1 (annoying), 2 (imposing), 3 (disruptive), 4 (damaging), and 5 (destructive). Every affected person should be assigned an individual score, since each one may suffer different degrees of harm. Even the dipsh*t deserves a score, because he or she is as likely as anyone to suffer a negative outcome.

Consider the case of Kenny Wells. His reward for the Atlanta airport debacle was ten years as a guest of the state. His outcome score would be 5 (destructive). People who were injured and required medical treatment would probably rate about 4 (damaging). Their outcome was quite bad, but not as devastating as Wells' decade in prison. They sustained non-life-threatening injuries, and their Thanksgiving plans were ruined. They also incurred involuntary expenses. The TSA agents, airport rebooking personnel in Atlanta and elsewhere, flight crews, air traffic controllers, and delayed passengers would all deserve individual scores based on the level of distress they experienced.

How would you rate my post-concert fiasco in the parking lot? Some might consider it a 1 (annoying), but I place it at 2 (imposing), for both my date and myself. We both were lost, concerned for our safety, weary from searching for my car, and uncertain how we would ever find it. That's more than a mere annoyance.

Here is an illustration that represents the complete analytical scheme:

Dipsh*t Analytics

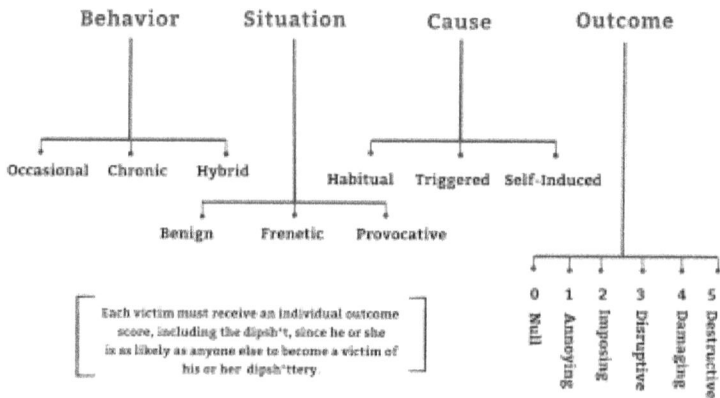

Behavior   Situation   Cause   Outcome

Occasional Chronic Hybrid   Habitual Triggered Self-Induced

Benign Frenetic Provocative

Each victim must receive an individual outcome score, including the dipsh*t, since he or she is as likely as anyone else to become a victim of his or her dipsh*ttery

0 1 2 3 4 5
Null Annoying Imposing Disruptive Damaging Destructive

Here are these analytics applied to yet another case. Writing for *The Paris Review,* Halle Butler provided the following vignette in her article, "One Word: Dipsh*t." Butler describes the obnoxious behavior of a woman on a commercial flight traveling with her two children.

> She had a very loud, affected voice…"Asher, if you wish it, you may have one of your Laffy Taffys now, but then only two Laffy Taffys will remain." How elegant! The kid didn't respond, didn't care either way, but she kept pushing them on him as if it were some kind of Stanford marshmallow experiment. Every time she said something, she repeated it (once more for the balcony!). Of course, she read to them, at top volume…glancing from side to side to see if we noticed how good she was at this.
>
> Meanwhile, the kids tuned her out to play video games and eat wads of candy.
>
> When the plane was descending, she was like, "The flight to Manhattan is not all that long, if you recall the flight to London. Do you recall when we flew to London? That was a much longer flight than this…You may have another Laffy Taffy if you wish." At that point, the guy across the aisle closed his eyes, exhaled, and said, very softly, "Jesus f***ing Christ."

How should we apply dipsh*t analytics to this overly dramatic paragon of motherhood? Lacking any additional information about her, I'll classify her as an occasional type. Someone as clueless and inconsiderate as this woman could very well be a chronic type, but I'll give her the benefit of the doubt. (In a later chapter you'll learn a rule for classifying dipsh*ts when you don't know their history. But let's not cross that bridge just yet.)

The situation prevailing at that time (i.e., traveling on a commercial flight) was benign. She was not dealing with any extenuating circumstances. Likewise, it seems that nothing triggered her. And while this kind of narcissistic behavior could have been habitual, it strikes me as self-induced. I think she probably chose this occasion to call attention to herself more than she might ordinarily. Perhaps she saw an opportunity to show off and took full advantage of it.

Finally, I place her outcome rating (i.e., how she affected her fellow passengers) at level 1 (annoying). She was obnoxious, but no real harm was done. Her own outcome rating is 0 (null), because she suffered no adverse consequences as a result of her preening. Here's a summary of my ratings:

- **Behavior:** occasional
- **Situation:** benign
- **Cause:** self-induced
- **Outcome:** 1 (annoying) for passengers; 0 (null) for Mommy Dearest.

Onward to Disaster!

Now follow along as I apply our analytical scheme to some cases ripped ever so gently from the headlines:

The Cookie Monster. In the Orlando, Florida suburb of Altamonte Springs, Amari Bente Hendricks, age 24, allegedly brandished a gun at a McDonald's drive-thru when employees refused to give her a free cookie. (I hasten to add that she is innocent until proven guilty.) According to the news site, Law & Crime,

Hendricks continued ranting and raving even after the store manager relented and gave her a cookie.

Still not satisfied, Hendricks left her vehicle and headed for the restaurant's entrance. Employees scurried to lock the doors before she could get inside, but she was too fast for them. She fought with an employee who was trying to lock her out, causing him minor injuries. Hendricks finally fled the scene, but police caught up with her a few blocks away. They charged her with aggravated assault, battery, and resisting arrest. She denied threatening anyone with her gun, but police said that surveillance video showed her "holding a dark colored object similar to the shape of a firearm in her right hand."

Dipsh*t analytics:

- **Behavior:** chronic (Low flashpoint and extreme overreaction.)
- **Situation:** benign (Drive-thru was not frenetic until she made it so; cookie was trivial.)
- **Cause:** triggered (Possibly a habitual type, but I'll give her the benefit of the doubt.)
- **Outcome:** 4 (destructive) for employees and also for the cookie monster herself; 2 (imposing) for the police, prosecutor, and the court.

Cycle of Abuse. In 2000, Olympian Marty Northstein won the gold medal in cycling. He took home the silver in 1996. Fast forward to today and Northstein, a former county commissioner, stands convicted of "defiant trespass," a third-class misdemeanor.

He pleaded guilty to resolve charges that he stalked his former girlfriend and her new boyfriend.

Prosecutors alleged that Northstein perpetrated "a nearly year-long [*sic*] campaign of harassment by driving past their homes, damaging their cars, sending anonymous letters with vulgar sexual references, and attempting to smear the boyfriend with false accusations of sexual misconduct." Northstein was sentenced to 12 months of probation and mental health counseling. The judge barred him from contacting either of the victims.

Dipsh*t analytics:

- **Behavior:** hybrid (He was a high achiever but out of control, stalking-wise.)
- **Situation:** benign (The breakup may have been provocative, but it didn't last all year.)
- **Cause:** triggered (By the breakup and his ex's new relationship.)
- **Outcome:** 5 (destructive) for the victims, 4 (damaging) for Northstein; 2 (imposing) for the police, prosecutor, and the court.

Burning bush. Apparently the concept of a "tree of life" holds some reverence among Latter-Day Saints. In a suburb of the Mormon stronghold of Salt Lake City, 38-year-old Crystal Nicole Moss reportedly set a "tree of life" ablaze in her apartment. At first it refused to catch fire, so she allegedly doused it with alcohol. The fire quickly raged out of control, whereupon Moss took her dog and left the apartment. According to police, she made no attempt to alert her neighbors that the building was on fire. When first responders arrived, she reportedly confessed to police that "she was trying to burn away the negative energy, sadness and pain her in life." No one was injured, but the property damage was severe. Several tenants were displaced. Moss faces trial for arson.

Dipsh*t analysis:

- **Behavior:** occasional (As far as we know; in a later chapter I'll present a rule for dealing with uncertainty in analyzing behavior.)
- **Situation:** benign (She may have been in distress about her personal problems, but no immediate external circumstances induced her to start an indoor fire.)
- **Cause:** triggered (By her own personal problems.)
- **Outcome:** 5 (destructive) for Moss, for the displaced tenants, and for the building's owner; 2 (imposing) for firefighters, the police, prosecutor, and court.

Latter-Day Ain't. Police in Farmington, Utah pulled over 25-year-old Chase Allan for having a suspicious license plate on his car. Allan, a so-called "sovereign citizen," apparently subscribed to the belief that he was exempt from obeying traffic laws. In bodycam video, Allan is heard telling the officer, "I don't need [vehicle] registration and I don't answer questions." Allan reportedly refused to present identification and argued with the officer. He finally did present some form of ID, which the cop seemed to believe was a "fake passport," according to the video.

Additional officers arrived on the scene and the decision was made to remove Allan from his vehicle, presumably for an arrest. He adamantly refused to get out. At some point police became aware that Allan was wearing a holstered pistol. The website Law & Crime reported that "Allan's hand can be seen moving toward his right hip, where the holster is located. It is also apparent from the video that Allan is wearing his seatbelt, and the buckle is located near his right hip as well." An officer yelled, "Gun! Gun! Gun!" Five officers opened fire, and Allan reportedly died on the scene.

Dipsh*t analytics:

- **Behavior:** hybrid (I'm taking the generous view that his dipsh*ttery was limited to his sovereign citizen delusions.)
- **Situation:** frenetic (A traffic stop can be stressful and may end with a ticket, but it is not provocative unless either the citizen or the officer behaves outrageously. This situation was not provocative until Allan made it so.)
- **Cause:** triggered (By Allan's delusional beliefs and problems with authority.)
- **Outcome:** 5 (destructive) for Allan and his family; 4 (damaging) for police officers who must live with having killed him in response to his obstinate obstruction.

Hydration Blues. In the movie, *Star Trek V: The Final Frontier*, a rogue Vulcan hijacks the Enterprise to a planet where he expects to meet God. When the landing party beams down, "God" demands that they give him the Enterprise. At this point, Captain Kirk asks, "What does God need with a starship?" That scene came to mind when I read about a couple of Alabama Einsteins arrested for allegedly digging up and stealing a fire hydrant. *What do two dipsh*ts need with a fire hydrant?*

According to WALA television in Mobile, a passing motorist observed Keith Haley, age 43, and Karla Frye, 39, removing the hydrant, and notified police. The cops soon spotted the suspects' vehicle and pulled them over. Along with the hydrant, officers reportedly found the criminal masterminds in possession of guns and drugs.

Dipsh*t analytics:

- **Behavior:** chronic (How could it be otherwise with these two?)
- **Situation:** benign (Surely the hydrant was minding its own business.)
- **Cause:** self-induced
- **Outcome:** 4 (damaging) for the two master criminals, since they will probably be ordered to pay a fine, make restitution, and complete probation (but the outcome is 5 if either gets sent to big-boy or big-girl prison); 3 (disruptive) for the city, since they have to replace the hydrant; 2 (imposing) for cops, the prosecutor, and the court.

The Ten Laws

Dipsh*t analytics will allow you to size up any person of that ilk you're likely to encounter. To further explain dipsh*ts as a class of humanity as well as the reasons for their behavior, I submit for your consideration the *Ten Laws of Dipsh*ttery*. Each chapter that follows is devoted to one of these laws:

1. Inside every person is a dipsh*t trying to get out.

2. Underestimate the destructive potential of dipsh*ts at your own peril.

3. Although sometimes unavoidable, it is always a mistake to interact with dipsh*ts.

4. When in doubt always assume that a dipsh*t is the chronic type unless there is good reason to believe otherwise.

5. A dipsh*t is as likely as anyone else to be his or her own victim.

6. Whom the gods wish to destroy, they first make a dipsh*t.

7. Do not attribute to malice that which can be explained by dipsh*ttery alone.

8. As dipsh*ts increase numerically, dipsh*ttery multiplies exponentially.

9. Any well-meaning attempt to intervene with a dipsh*t is likely to result in the intervention itself devolving into dipsh*ttery (see third law).

10. Dipsh*ttery is a force of nature which can neither be eradicated nor avoided.

Please note law number four in particular. So far I've made informed guesses about whether the dipsh*ts in this chapter are the occasional, chronic, or hybrid types. Now that you've been introduced to law number 4, I will no longer speculate. Except when there's good reason to conclude otherwise, I will classify them as chronic. So should you. When in doubt, assume the worst of dipsh*ts.

And so, dear reader, you have reached the end of chapter one. If you wish you may now have one of your Laffy Taffys. But then only two Laffy Taffys will remain.

* * *

"Higher than the beasts, lower than the angels, stuck in our idiot
Eden."
– Ford Madox Ford

Chapter Two

The First Law of Dipsh*ttery: Inside Every Person is a Dipsh*t Trying to Get Out

Remember Richard Kazmaier, the biologist who pleaded guilty to importing "skulls, skeletons, and taxidermy mounts" of protected wildlife in violation of the Lacey Act? He drew a six-month sentence, a $5000 fine, and probation. Except for his numerous Lacey Act violations, Kazmaier functioned as a successful biology professor for many years. Even in the best of us, there is a dipsh*t yearning to break free. (Mine certainly cut loose the night of that ill-fated concert date.)

Consider the case of former Indiana State Police trooper, Brian L. Hamilton. During traffic stops, Hamilton made a practice of questioning motorists about their salvation and church attendance. He also passed out religious literature. At least two drivers didn't appreciate being detained for more than just a traffic stop and filed lawsuits against him.

Hamilton's supervisors admonished him to knock off the proselytizing. When he didn't, they fired him. Afterwards, Hamilton told a reporter, "Oh well…I'm just following what the Lord told me to do and you can't change what the Lord tells you to do. So if the Lord tells me to speak about Jesus Christ, I do. And that's why they fired me, so that's where we're at."

Some people might assume that Hamilton was delusional in assuming he could preach to detained motorists in his capacity as a peace officer. Others might conclude that he was obsessed with proselytizing. Neither of those explanations quite fit Hamilton's behavior in my opinion. His stubborn refusal to keep his religious beliefs separate from his official duties is an example of what 19th century psychiatrist, Carl Wernicke, called an *over-valued idea*.

A *delusion* is a false belief that no amount of contrary evidence can overcome. For example, even today some people believe the earth is flat, and they cannot be convinced otherwise. An *obsession* is a persistent, unwanted, intrusive thought, and it's *ego-dystonic* (i.e., displeasing to oneself). Overvalued ideas consist of otherwise benign thoughts that have become warped by intense belief and by limited introspection and self-control.

Unlike obsessive thoughts, over-valued ideas are *ego-syntonic* – that is, pleasing to the individual. These are the characteristics of an over-valued idea: (i) an intense belief which in moderation would be considered conventional or plausible; (ii) the thoughts are persistent and pleasing; (iii) the ideas or beliefs arise from an individual's unique personality, experiences, and culture; and (iv) the thoughts would seem extreme but not bizarre to an observer.

Hamilton's religious faith would not be considered abnormal, especially in the United States, except that he used the power of his badge to force religion on unwilling motorists. His over-valued idea motivated him to preach, perhaps even to the level of a compulsion. But having a compulsion does not give anyone carte blanche to inflict distress on others. If Hamilton had an irresistible urge, it was his responsibility to manage it or to seek professional help.

There is no indication that Hamilton's evangelizing persisted throughout his entire 14-year career with the Indiana State Police. And tellingly, he didn't preach to his fellow troopers. Otherwise, his employer would have known of his inappropriate workplace conduct long before any motorists complained. As with many religious extremists, it seems that Hamilton used the excuse of "I'm just following God's orders" as cover to do as he pleased, regardless of the rights of others.

Now let's apply dipsh*t analytics to the proselytizing patrolman:

- **Behavior:** hybrid (Pursuant to the fourth law, I'd go with "chronic," but we have good reason to believe that he was a mostly responsible individual except for his roadside homilies.)

- **Situation:** benign (A routine traffic stop may be frenetic for the motorist, but not for an officer who feels comfortable enough to engage the driver in religious conversation.)

- **Cause:** self-induced (By his over-valued idea.)

- **Outcome:** 4 (damaging) for Hamilton, since his proselytizing got him fired; 2 or 3 (imposing or disruptive) for motorists, depending on each person's level of discomfort with Hamilton's behavior; 2 (imposing) for the supervisory officers who had to deal with his misconduct and ultimately terminate Hamilton.

Both Kazmaier and Hamilton are hybrid types – seemingly respectable, upstanding citizens who allowed their inner dipsh*t to run riot in one area of their lives. Or consider the three Georgia men who chased down Ahmaud Arbery, a 25-year-old black man, as he jogged through their suburban neighborhood. Gregory McMichael, 65, Travis McMichael, 35, and their neighbor William "Roddie" Bryan, 52, were convicted of murder, committing a hate crime, and several other felonies related to the incident.

Arbery loitered briefly at a construction site in the defendants' neighborhood but did not steal or disturb anything. As he continued jogging, the defendants in two pickup trucks stalked and attempted to detain him. Prosecutors pointed out at trial that the white men had no reasonable basis to suspect Arbery of wrongdoing, nor did they have any right to hunt him down, harass him, or kill him. The men had a history of racially charged statements, and the entire incident seems to have been an almost hysterical reaction to seeing an unknown black man running in the street.

Dipsh*ttery is an inadequate term to characterize the barbaric behavior of these men toward Arbery. Their brutality merits the most damning rebuke. But it is their stupid and despicable belligerence that set the tragic sequence of events in motion. Their extreme, knee-jerk response to a black stranger "on their turf" prompted them to act like vigilantes, without any reasonable cause to do so.

Before I present my analysis of these cretins, I feel the need to make full disclosure. I am a native Georgian myself. I grew up just a couple of hours from where Arbery was killed. I didn't know his killers, but I've known many Southern rednecks of that type. As a boy I witnessed Southern whites attack blacks during the non-violent protests of the civil rights era. It's shocking in the 21st century to realize that there are still Southern whites who harbor that same spirit of unprovoked bigotry and animosity toward blacks who are just minding their own business.

Dipsh*t analytics for the Georgia Goobers:

- **Behavior:** hybrid (I'd dearly love to tag these three as chronic, but from all appearances their lives were normal aside from their reactionary racism.)
- **Situation:** benign (Arbery did not incite these vigilantes.)
- **Cause:** self-induced (Their own racism led them to unleash mayhem.)
- **Outcome:** 5 (destructive) for Arbery and his family and likewise for Arbery's attackers and their families; 2 (imposing) for the police, prosecutor, judge, and jury; 3 (disruptive) for the Georgia community where this happened.

What Fools These Dipsh*ts Be

Psychologist Stephen Greenspan has developed a method of deconstructing dipsh*ttery (what he calls "foolish actions") based on four influencing factors: *situation, cognition, personality,* and *affect/state.* External circumstances and influences that cause or contribute to foolish actions make up the situation. This is the only factor that isn't inherent in the individual. Cognition consists of an individual's thoughts, feelings, beliefs, and conclusions in response to the situation. Personality includes temperament, attitudes, psychological problems (if any), and character traits (e.g., dishonesty, impulsiveness, tolerance, generosity, etc.). Finally, affect/state consists of one's current biological status – enraged, intoxicated, anxious, or weakened by illness, for example.

When foolish actions occur, Greenspan maintains that the four factors in combination provide the underlying explanation. Greenspan's model gives us another way to evaluate and understand obtuse, obnoxious behavior.

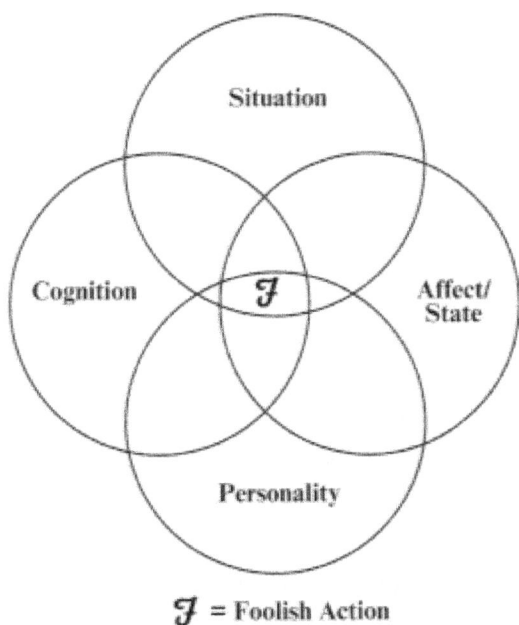

$\mathcal{F}$ = Foolish Action

Greenspan's four-factor model of foolishness

Consider the unfortunate case of former congressman, Anthony Weiner. The New York politician resigned from Congress in 2011 amid revelations that he had sent naked pictures of himself to various women. In 2013 Weiner attempted a come-back by running for mayor of New York. That summer, journalists reported that Weiner, using the alias "Carlos Danger," had continued to send explicit photos to women after his resignation from Congress. Weiner's political future imploded amid the ensuing outrage. His campaign manager resigned, and the disgraced candidate won only 4.9% of the vote in the Democratic primary. In 2019 Weiner pleaded guilty to sending obscene material to a minor. He drew a 21-month sentence and was released in 2021.

One of the women Weiner corresponded with stated that he described himself as "an argumentative, perpetually horny middle-aged man." In these words we see confirmation of the driven, hyper-sexual tendencies that motivated his self-destructive behavior. But being a Type A personality doesn't give Weiner a free pass, nor does being a horndog. These are character flaws that need to be recognized and managed, not indulged.

Weiner threw away a promising political career because he failed to control his impulses. He damaged himself, his family, and his constituents, plummeting from a seat in Congress to a cell in prison. We know little about when, how many times, or with whom he committed lewd acts. An analysis of Weiner's dipsh*ttery requires that we speculate about these unknown details. But let's give it a try.

Dipsh*t analytics:

- **Behavior:** hybrid (His recklessness was limited to his sex life.)
- **Situation:** benign? (Presumably he sexted when circumstances were calm and private.)

- **Cause:** self-induced (By his failure to control his sexual urges.)
- **Outcome:** 5 (destructive) for Weiner and his family; 4 (damaging) for his campaign staff and donors; 3 (disruptive) for his constituents; 2 (imposing) for the police, prosecutor, and criminal justice system.
- Here's a four-factor analysis of Weiner's foolishness based on Greenspan's model:
- **Situation:** benign? (Same as above.)
- **Cognition:** We don't know what he was thinking. Perhaps he was using the wrong part of his anatomy for that purpose.
- **Personality:** Weiner reportedly described himself as "argumentative" and "perpetually horny." Given that he engaged in high-risk sexual shenanigans despite being a well-known elected official, we may conclude that he is impulsive, a risk-taker, and sometimes does not use good judgment.
- **Aspect/state:** Both the circumstances and his own words peg him as a constant horndog. Beyond that, we don't know what was going on with him physiologically at the time.

As Weiner's case illustrates, it's difficult to apply Greenspan's four-factor model without having complete information. I won't use it again for that reason. But it is an excellent model for analyzing foolishness when there is sufficient data. Dipsh*t analytics is easier to apply, even when a few details are missing.

Making Sense of Senselessness: Some Theories

Danny Lemoi, an "ivermectin influencer," died in 2023 from an enlarged heart. The 50-year-old Rhode Island man reportedly took veterinary-grade ivermectin, a dewormer for horses and cattle, every day for the past decade. On the morning of March 3rd, he posted on social media, "HAPPY FRIDAY ALL YOU POISONOUS HORSE PASTE EATING SURVIVORS !!!" A few hours later he was found dead.

Heart damage is one of many side effects attributed to ingestion of ivermectin in large doses intended for livestock. Lemoi recommended high-dose ivermectin to his followers on social media and instructed them on how to treat children with the drug. His qualifications for giving medical advice were apparently limited to his expertise as "a heavy equipment operator." According to Vice.com, many of his followers now suffer from ivermectin's side effects.

You may have noticed that all the cases I've presented so far in this chapter are hybrid types. Lemoi also fits that profile. These examples illustrate the truth of the first law – that "inside every person is a dipsh*t trying to get out." These otherwise ordinary and functional individuals have allowed their behavior to wreak havoc in one area of their lives.

Lemoi's ivermectin-laced dipsh*t analysis:

- **Behavior:** hybrid
- **Situation:** benign
- **Cause:** self-induced

- **Outcome:** 5 (destructive) for Lemoi and his family; 5 (destructive) for his followers who have experienced ivermectin side-effects; 4 (damaging) for his followers who have not yet manifested adverse symptoms.

There are many theoretical models that can aid our analysis and understanding of senseless behavior. One of the most well-known is the *Dunning-Kruger effect*. It describes a tendency of individuals with limited skill or knowledge in a particular area to overestimate their competence. They mistakenly believe they are more capable than they really are. Lemoi's ivermectin advocacy stands as a glaring example.

The Dunning-Kruger effect is a type of cognitive bias. Psychologists David Dunning and Justin Kruger explored this paradoxical behavior in a 1999 study. They found that people who scored in the bottom quartile on tests of humor, grammar, and logic tended to overestimate their abilities, while those who scored in the top quartile were prone to underestimate their abilities.

Clearly, Danny Lemoi exceeded his knowledge when he assumed the role of "ivermectin influencer" and advised gullible podcast listeners to ingest a dangerous form of the drug. The Georgia pickup truck posse who pursued Ahmaud Arbery vastly overestimated their right to act as vigilantes and underestimated Arbery's right not to be hunted down and killed in the street. And ex-trooper Hamilton seriously overplayed the "I'm on a mission from God" excuse as justification for his official misconduct.

In 1976, Carlo M. Cipolla, a professor of economic history, developed his now-famous "Basic Laws of Human Stupidity." These laws allow us to classify people according to the harm they cause for themselves and for others. In that way, Cipolla's five laws of stupidity align well with dipsh*t analytics and the Ten Laws of Dipsh*ttery presented in this and later chapters.

Cipolla's Basic Laws of Human Stupidity

• **First law:** "Always and inevitably, everyone underestimates the number of stupid individuals in circulation."
• **Second law:** "The probability that a certain person [is] stupid is independent of any other characteristic of that person.'
• **Third ("golden") law:** "A stupid person is a person who causes losses to another person or to a group of persons while himself deriving no gain and even possibly incurring losses."
• **Fourth law:** "Non-stupid people always underestimate the damaging power of stupid individuals. In particular, non-stupid people constantly forget that at all times and places, and under any circumstances, to deal and/or associate with stupid people always turns out to be a costly mistake."
• **Fifth law:** "A stupid person is the most dangerous type of person."

Cipolla grouped people into four categories – *helpless, intelligent, stupid,* and *bandits.* A helpless person is someone who harms himself while benefiting others. People who fall victim to Ponzi schemes or romance scams are familiar examples. An intelligent person engages in win/win transactions, such as agreeing to repair someone's vacation home in exchange for permission to occupy the home for several weeks. A stupid person harms both himself and others (which corresponds to our definition of a dipsh*t). Bandits require further explanation, because there are two kinds.

Bandits, like Cipolla's stupid people, also qualify as dipsh*ts. They cause harm to others and in the long run to themselves since banditry is an unsustainable, dead-end activity. Just ask Bernard Madoff. But unlike those whom Cipolla classifies as stupid, bandits gain a temporary benefit until they get caught. Stupid people in contrast sustain immediate losses.

One kind of bandit derives greater benefits for himself than the losses caused to his victim. For example, someone who steals asthma medicine from a pharmacy for a sick child acquires a much greater benefit than the business's small economic loss. We might even desire leniency for this kind of thief. The second kind of bandit, however, causes a greater loss to his victim than the benefit he or she receives. A dipsh*t who steals a car only to crash it a short time later during a police chase is a bandit of the second kind.

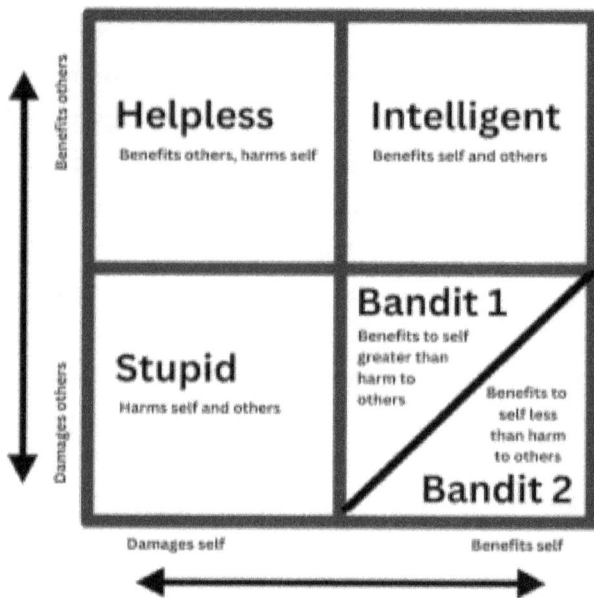

Cipolla's classification of intelligent versus stupid behavior

Here are some examples that illustrate the overlap of Cipolla's laws and dipsh*t analytics:

Stupid + Dipsh*t: Video surveillance led to the arrest of 31-year-old Charles Sutherland, a Maryland school librarian, for allegedly spray-painting "groomer" on public library buildings. Police searched his home and found child pornography on his computer, according to WTOP news radio. The station also reported that "Police also found diapers and dolls around his apartment, including a child-sized doll in his bed. Sutherland is alleged to have told police that he had no children, and no nieces or nephews."

Under Cipolla's laws, Sutherland would qualify for the stupid category. His criminal misconduct harmed both himself and others. This is his profile based on dipsh*t analysis:

- **Behavior:** chronic (With charges of both vandalism and child pornography pending against him, Sutherland's alleged criminality affects more than one aspect of his life.)
- **Situation:** benign (No external factors provoked his criminal acts.)
- **Cause:** self-induced (Given the senselessness of his alleged crimes, Sutherland could qualify as a habitual type, but I've given him the benefit of the doubt. Dipsh*ttery is self-induced if it's not habitual and not immediately triggered by some provocation.)
- **Outcome:** 5 (destructive) for Sullivan; 4 (damaging) for the libraries he vandalized; 2 (imposing) for the police, prosecutor, and court; 4 (damaging) for child porn victims if they become aware that Sutherland possessed of images of their abuse; if Sutherland himself sexually abused any children, their outcome score would be 5 (destructive).

Type 1 Bandit + Dipsh*t: The first type of bandit obtains a greater benefit for him- or herself than any loss caused to the victim. In the summer of 2021, a group of thieves in England broke into a Liverpool car dealership and stole over $1.3 million worth of luxury cars, including several Audi, BMW, and Mercedes-Benz models. They entered by breaking a skylight and lowering themselves into the showroom with ropes. Next, they disabled the dealership's security system and loaded the cars onto a getaway truck. The stolen cars were sold on the black market for more than their sticker price, with some of them being shipped out of the country.

Type 1 bandits are rare. Typically, victims suffer losses equal to or greater than the bandit's gain, which places the perpetrator in the type 2 category. Here are the dipsh*t analytics of the luxury car thieves:

- **Behavior:** chronic (These probably weren't first-time offenders; when it doubt – chronic.)
- **Situation:** benign (Most likely, the cars were minding their own business.)
- **Cause:** habitual (Assuming these were professional thieves.)
- **Outcome:** 4 (damaging) for the dealership; 0 (null) for the thieves if they got away with this crime, or 5 (destructive) if they were caught, convicted, and sent to prison; 0 (null) for their buyers if they suffered no repercussions for buying stolen cars, but 4 or 5 (damaging or destructive) if they were caught and punished (rating depends on severity of their punishment).

Type 2 Bandit + Dipsh*t. Mario Hehr, 30, and Alexandra Gaiswinkler, 27, stand accused of stealing $40,000 worth of power tools from various Home Depot stores in Colorado and pawning them for less than they were worth. Upon entering each store, Hehr would select a large trash bin and fill it up with tools.

He didn't hesitate to cut theft-prevention security cables whenever they interfered with his heist. When his bin was fully loaded, Hehr would waltz out of the store and load his bounty into a getaway van, police said. Gaiswinkler reportedly accompanied him and remained in the van. In all, Hehr is believed to have boosted 199 items from five Home Depots.

If the allegations against them are true, Hehr and Gaiswinkler qualify both as dipsh*ts and as type 2 bandits. The losses they caused to Home Depot were greater than the ill-gotten profits they received. I should clarify by stating that they were type 2 bandits in the short-run, because their crime wave was brief and their profits paltry. In the long-run they were stupid-dipsh*ts, because their thievery harmed both Home Depot and themselves. Behold their dipsh*t analysis:

- **Behavior:** chronic (When in doubt, chronic.)
- **Situation:** benign (If they were addicts desperate to buy drugs or trying to score rent money to avoid eviction, I might rate the situation as "frenetic." But I don't know that.)
- **Cause:** habitual (Who else would commit serial crimes while under video surveillance?)
- **Outcome:** 5 (destructive) for the alleged criminals; 3 (disruptive) for Home Depot; 2 (imposing) for the police, prosecutor, and court.

In November of 2021 Amy Hall and Ricki Collin livestreamed themselves entering an Oregon cookie store without face masks. At the time there was a statewide mask mandate in force for all commercial establishments. When the store's owner confronted the pair and asked them to mask up or leave, they argued with her and then assaulted her. The entire incident appeared to be a stunt to gain social media attention, and these troublemakers recorded the video evidence that would be used against them.

Police arrested Hall and Collin shortly after they left the store. Their victim was taken to the hospital. Once he scored bail, Collin went on the lam. There is an active warrant for his arrest. Meanwhile, Hall went to trial and was convicted of "assault, criminal trespass, harassment, burglary, and disorderly conduct." At sentencing, the store's owner testified about her struggle to recover from the senseless violence and the humiliation of her assault going viral on social media. When given a chance to speak, Hall showed no remorse. She maintained that COVID-19 was "BS" and blamed the court for her conviction. "I'm the only innocent one here in this room," she said.

The judge called her a bully and pointed out that her own dipsh*t video was all the proof the jury needed to find her guilty. He sentenced her to 46 months in prison followed by three years' probation.

Cipolla would certainly classify this pair as stupid. They "sowed the wind and reaped the whirlwind," but their stupid stunt also unleashed havoc on the hapless store owner. The gravity of their violence is underscored by the fact that the incident was meaningless, cruel, and devoid of any beneficial purpose. These contemptible cretins exemplify the principle that everyone has an inner dipsh*t desperately trying to break free – except that these two aided and abetted in the escape.

Dipsh*t analytics for Hall and Collin:

- **Behavior:** chronic
- **Situation:** benign
- **Cause:** habitual
- **Outcome:** 5 (destructive) for Hall and Collin; 5 (destructive) for the store owner because of her physical injuries and lasting psychological trauma; 2 (imposing) for the police, prosecutor, and court.

Clearly, Hall and Collin manifest the Dunning-Kruger effect. Upon entering the store unmasked, they began arguing with the owner about the legality of the statewide mask mandate. And as mask scofflaws themselves, they assumed that they knew more about the pandemic than public health officials. Even at her trial, Hall remained dismissive of COVID-19, calling it "BS." They may also have fallen victim to the *Lake Wobegon effect*.

In Garrison Keillor's fictional hometown of Lake Wobegon, "all the women are strong, all the men are good-looking, and all the children are above average." The Lake Wobegon effect, also called *illusory superiority*, is a self-perception bias similar to the Dunning-Kruger effect, but with one key difference. The Lake Wobegon effect describes a tendency to rate one's knowledge and abilities higher than the same qualities in other people, while the Dunning-Kruger effect indicates over-confidence about one's knowledge and skill without comparison to others. Hall seemed to manifest illusory superiority at sentencing when she accused the court of operating illegally, continued to profess that COVID-

19 is a hoax, and claimed to be the only innocent person in the courtroom.

If you've ever tried to argue rationally with people who hold irrational beliefs, you know they can be immune to evidence and logic. I grew up among people in the South who believed that the Bible is literally and historically factual. As I matured and began to shed those beliefs, I saw that it was useless to point out that Noah, for example, could not have gotten penguins and kangaroos onto the ark. If the Genesis accounts of creation and Noah's flood were true, there would be fossils of giraffes, woodpeckers, and velociraptors in the same geologic layers. There aren't, because those species are separated by millions of years of evolution. But for biblical literalists, questioning their faith could unravel their entire belief system, leaving them untethered from reality as they understand it.

This tendency of people to double-down on irrational beliefs when confronted with contrary evidence is known as the *backfire effect*. Some people will cling to what they believe, even against overwhelming proof, rather than deal with the cognitive dissonance that would result from admitting they were wrong. In Amy Hall's case, the more she was confronted with evidence of her guilt and false beliefs, the tighter she held on to her entrenched irrationality.

A Toxic Trifecta: Hubris, Arrogance, and Narcissism

Jonathan Nakhla, age 38, sits in jail convicted of reckless murder. Drunk and driving 138 miles per hour on a service road in Mobile, Alabama, Nakhla crashed his Audi convertible. The vehicle reportedly rolled six times before coming to a stop. He survived, but his passenger, 24-year-old Samantha Thomas, died in the crash. The posted speed limit was 45 miles per hour.

So, is Nakhla some inbred, semi-literate Alabama redneck? On the contrary, he was a neurosurgeon until his reckless driving cost him his medical license, his career, and his freedom. Nakhla, a man of intelligence, skill, and discipline, allowed his inner dipsh*t to turn deadly. According to the Law & Crime website, he "bragged about his fast driving and…used a badge and ID card, which were given to him as a volunteer police surgeon, to get out of tickets." At this writing, he remains in jail awaiting sentencing.

Dipsh*t analytics for the neurosurgeon from hell:

- **Behavior:** hybrid (Only one area of his life manifests stupid, despicable behavior.)
- **Situation:** benign (He was drunk and his street racing was high-pressure, but those circumstances didn't exist until he created them.)
- **Cause:** self-induced
- **Outcome:** 5 (destructive) for Nakhla and Thomas; 5 (destructive) for their families; 2 (imposing) for first-responders at the crash site; 2 (imposing) for the police, prosecutor, and court dealing with him post-arrest.

While we can't peer into Nakhla's mind, testimony at trial revealed that he drank excessively and then chose to drive. He reportedly bragged about frequently speeding and getting away with it. And even allowing for his drunkenness, 138 miles per hour on a city street is outrageous.

Based on the above information, it's not unreasonable to conclude that Nakhla felt invincible and immune to consequences. After all, he had conquered one of the most challenging fields of study, namely medicine. He was a physician – and not just any doctor, but a neurosurgeon. If he did indulge his feelings of invulnerability, this would indicate that he fell under the spell of *narcissistic immunity*, the belief that one is exempt from facing consequences.

In Greek myth, Bellerophon tamed winged Pegasus and rode him into battle against the three-headed Chimaera. After slaying the monster, Bellerophon felt all-powerful. He believed himself entitled to fly Pegasus to the summit of Mount Olympus and meet the gods. Offended by Bellerophon's arrogance, the gods sent a fly to sting Pegasus. The horse bucked and Bellerophon plummeted to earth. But he didn't die. The angry gods weren't finished with him yet. Instead, Bellerophon was crippled and spent his remaining years searching in vain for his long-lost Pegasus.

Similar warnings have come down to us since antiquity. A recurrent character in Greek tragedies is the hero who embodies a fatal flaw that makes his doom inevitable. In Chaucer's *Canterbury Tales*, a monk recounts how Lucifer, Julius Caesar, and others met their downfall because of pride or arrogance. Shakespeare's *Richard III* and *MacBeth* dramatize the bitter lessons of hubris, narcissism, and power lust. Mary Shelley's *Frankenstein* cautions against the vanity of abusing technology to achieve portentous results that cannot be controlled (a lesson we never seem to learn).

In this chapter you've seen cases of self-love, self-interest, and self-aggrandizement spinning out of control and becoming pathological. Dipsh*ttery soon follows as a character flaw that bursts though like a flood when the dam breaks. An arrogant, overweening dipsh*t of this kind is a different breed than those who act impulsively and seemingly out of character, or those who respond stupidly to some provocation. What they all have in common, however, is loss of control over their inner dipsh*t, whether momentarily or habitually.

Keeping our closeted demons contained requires that we apply a set of higher-order thinking skills. Fortunately, we have an array of countermeasures. That's true even if we're not presently aware of them.

For example, we know that good judgment is required when making decisions. But we may not be consciously aware that we're applying sophisticated cognitive abilities when we invest our money, plan an itinerary, or make healthy dietary choices, for example. Sound judgment is just one of our self-management skills. Another is cautiousness which counsels us to pause, to reflect, to take a deep breath, and to be still rather than to react.

At the end of this chapter (coming right up!), why not take a few minutes to write down your self-control skills which may rarely come to mind? In addition to good judgment, these might include self-discipline, patience, calmness under stress, willingness to shrug off provocations, and so on. This is your *anti-dipsh*t list*, and you get to decide what's on it. Keep it nearby while reading – or better yet, use it for a bookmark. The habits and abilities on your list will form the prison bars that keep your inner dipsh*t contained. They are your defensive tactics against the cretins you encounter.

As you progress through this book, consider adding more skills to your list as you become aware of them. Then review the list from time to time and reflect upon what you've written. As you read about the cases in later chapters, use your list to evaluate which higher-order skills could have prevented the disastrous outcomes.

In closing I'll leave you with the case of John Carter, age 36, a New Hampshire man, who was clocked doing 82 miles per hour on a street with a posted speed limit of 50. When a state trooper tried to pull him over, Carter stopped in the road, did a "burn-out," and then led the officer on a high-speed chase. He eventually crashed his truck and ran away but was apprehended. Police charged him with "operating after certification as a habitual offender, reckless conduct with a deadly weapon, possession of a controlled drug, dealing prescription drugs, resisting arrest, reckless operation of a motor vehicle, disobeying a police officer, and operating an unregistered motor vehicle."

Carter's mugshot shows him wearing a t-shirt with this message: "Didn't mean to offend you. That was just a bonus." And so, for his enthusiastic embodiment of the Granite State's motto,

"Live Free or Die," I hereby propose that Carter's jail cell be designated hereafter as the John Carter Memorial Bed and Breakfast. And I further recommend that a sign be hung above the cell door with these words: "Through these bars pass New Hampshire's greatest dipsh*ts."

* * *

"Sometimes I wonder whether the world is being run by smart people who are putting us on or by imbeciles who really mean it."

– Laurence J. Peter

Chapter Three

The Second Law: Underestimate the Destructive Potential of Dipsh*ts at Your Own Peril

On a fall day in 2022 retired Florida school principal, Tracey Nix, went to meet friends for lunch. She took her 7-month-old granddaughter, Uriel, along with her. Nix agreed to babysit Uriel that day, because the child's mother (Nix's daughter) had a beauty appointment.

Surveillance video reportedly showed Nix, age 65, strapping the baby into a car seat at about 1:40 p.m. as she prepared to drive home. Upon arriving there, Nix parked her SUV in the driveway and went inside to play the piano. Nix said that about three hours later she suddenly remembered that Uriel was still in the vehicle.

The temperature rose above 90°F (32°C) that day and would have been much higher in the unventilated vehicle. By the time Nix remembered Uriel, the baby was already dead. As tragic as this death is, it's only half the story. Eleven months earlier, Nix lost track of another grandchild who also died.

Previously, Uriel's mother had allowed Nix to babysit her other child, 16-month-old Ezra. According to news reports, Nix fell asleep on the sofa while watching Ezra. The toddler wandered off and found his way to a pond on the property where he drowned.

Kaila Nix, the children's mother, said that she struggled to trust her mother after Ezra's death, but ultimately decided that Uriel needed to have a relationship with her grandmother. So she forgave her mother and allowed her to care for Uriel. But after Uriel's death, Kaila insisted that her mother be criminally charged.

When Ezra died, authorities dismissed the matter as an unfortunate accident. However, Nix now stands accused of manslaughter in Uriel's death and is awaiting trial. Meanwhile, she has checked into a mental health facility and is said to have lapsed into an incommunicative state.

The Nix case and its needless infant fatalities illustrate the danger of underestimating the destructive power of dipsh*ts of the Tracey Nix persuasion. One accidental death may be a heartbreaking accident. A second accidental death is less than a year shows a stunning failure of competence, conscientiousness, and responsibility. Ezra's death apparently failed to serve as a wake-up call. Rather than becoming overly protective and hyper-vigilant with Uriel as one might expect in the wake of the previous tragedy, she allegedly forgot about her babysitting responsibilities for several hours. That level of nonchalance regarding the safety of her grandchildren constitutes stupid and despicable behavior.

Remember, Nix was a former school principal. She lacked neither intelligence nor education. In interviews, none of her relatives mentioned any medical issues that might have been mitigating factors in explaining her incompetence as a babysitter. In fact, her own daughter entrusted her repeatedly with the grandchildren. Something seems to be profoundly amiss in Nix's character. Most people would be more diligent in pet sitting a friend's cat or dog than she was in looking after her grandkids.

How would you rate Nix using dipsh*t analytics? Here's my assessment:

- **Behavior:** hybrid (Circumstantial evidence points to a mostly normal life except for her serial babysitting misadventures.)
- **Situation:** benign
- **Cause:** self-induced
- **Outcome:** 5 (destructive) for the infants, for Nix, and for her family members; 4 (damaging) for first responders who had to recover, investigate, and process the dead bodies of two babies; 2 (imposing) for police and the criminal justice system in prosecuting Nix.

Compare the Nix case with that of an Ohio woman who caused her dogs to attack a 6-year-old girl. Cassie Thierauf, age 38, lived on one side of a duplex, and the girl lived on the other side with her parents. The girl's mother reportedly caught Thierauf using drugs in their adjoining backyards and captured this on video. The mother then went inside to call the police. Meanwhile, the girl was playing in the front yard with neighborhood children.

The girl's father testified that "[Thierauf] called two dogs to attack four little girls who were out front. My 6-year-old [was] mauled by two of them while [Thierauf] stood there on her front porch watching." In a video played for the court, Thierauf can be heard yelling, "Your kids shouldn't have f****ed with me and my dogs." The girl suffered numerous bites to her face and body and had to undergo multiple surgeries. Thierauf pleaded guilty to child endangerment.

I rate Thierauf, the devil-dog neighbor, as follows:

- **Behavior:** chronic
- **Situation:** provocative (The victim's mother allegedly caught Thierauf doing drugs and began video recording; an argument ensued between the adults.)
- **Cause:** self-induced (If Thierauf had ordered the dogs to attack the child's mother, who was recording video, the cause would be "triggered." But there was nothing that triggered her to unleash the dogs against a child except her own spite.)
- **Outcome:** 5 (destructive) for child and her family and for Thierauf, who received a prison sentence; 2 (imposing) for the police and criminal justice system; 3 (disruptive) for the animal control officers who had to capture and euthanize the dogs.

Despite pleading guilty, Thierauf said during sentencing that she did not command the dogs to attack. She claimed that they slipped out when she left the door ajar. Judge Timothy Tepe dismissed that excuse as hogwash and sentenced her to two years in prison followed by two years of probation.

Nix and Thierauf both harmed young children. One lacked an apparent motive but seemingly yielded to repeated carelessness. The other acted maliciously and from spite. Unlike Nix's grandchildren, Thierauf's victim survived the attack, but is scarred physically and probably emotionally as well. In both cases the parents of the victimized children were also traumatized. Both of these women unleashed needless mayhem on children and their families, thereby securing for themselves a place of dishonor in the dipsh*t hall of infamy.

A Walk Through the Mental Landscape

It might come as no surprise that people with certain personality traits and psychological disorders can be prone to erratic or troublesome behavior. Even so, no one who is struggling with mental health challenges should be stigmatized because of their condition, just as we would not condemn people with influenza or arthritis for having those diseases. But having the flu doesn't give a sick person any special privilege to go around coughing on others, and having a mental disorder doesn't provide carte blanche for disruptive conduct.

Except for people who are mentally incompetent, we are all obligated to deal responsibly with our personal "issues." We must obey the law and avoid causing harm or distress to others. If we don't, we can expect to face the consequences. Competent people who allow their personal demons to run riot are fair game to be designated as dipsh*ts – and that's doubly true if they try to justify their toxic behavior by playing the mental health card.

The *Diagnostic and Statistical Manual of Mental Disorders, Fifth Edition* (DSM-5) is the Bible of psychological conditions relied upon by mental health professionals in the United States and Canada. Other countries use a similar diagnostic manual, the *International Classification of Diseases, Tenth Edition* (ICD-10). There are dozens of psychological disorders that could incentivize persons so afflicted to go full-tilt dipsh*t. But just as wanting to get drunk everyday does not make alcoholism a reasonable or desirable choice, neither does having a desire to misbehave excuse wreaking havoc.

A complete examination of DSM-5 disorders is not possible in this chapter, but the following selection of conditions and symptoms may prove insightful. Once again, stigmatizing mental health conditions is cruel and unethical. But having a basic understanding of certain disorders and their common symptoms can assist bystanders in putting toxic behavior in proper context when it does occur.

Personality Disorders

The DSM-5 organizes personality disorders into three groups: Cluster A, Cluster B, and Cluster C. The disorders in each cluster share similar traits and behavioral patterns.

Cluster A (odd or eccentric thoughts and behaviors) includes three diagnoses. Paranoid personality disorder (PPD) is characterized by chronic distrust and suspiciousness as well as a tendency to read hostile intent into the benign actions of others. Schizoid personality disorder (SPD) indicates people who are classic "loners." They show little interest in relationships with others. Schizotypal personality disorder (STPD) sufferers may have strange beliefs, distorted perceptions of reality, and bizarre thinking patterns. Because they appear odd to others, they have trouble establishing relationships and may have social anxiety because of it.

Cluster B (dramatic, erratic, or emotional thoughts and behaviors) consists of borderline personality disorder (BPD), narcissistic personality disorder (NPD), antisocial personality disorder

(ASPD), and histrionic personality disorder (HPD). These are sometimes referred to as "character disorders," because people in this cluster can manifest toxic behavior in their relationships.

People with BPD experience intense and unstable emotions, struggle with a fragile self-image, and fear abandonment. They find it difficult to maintain stable relationships. Borderlines are also prone to impulsive, irresponsible behavior.

Narcissists have a grandiose sense of self-importance, a preoccupation with fantasies of unlimited success, and a lack of empathy. This extreme self-centeredness masks a fragile ego. People with NPD expect uncritical admiration and exhibit a sense of entitlement. In their view, other people are exploitable and disposable as necessary to meet the narcissist's expectations.

ASPD is the clinical term for sociopathy. Characterized by disregard for the rights of others and a lack of empathy, individuals with ASPD engage in manipulative or deceitful behavior, act impulsively, and violate social norms. A diagnosis of conduct disorder during childhood is common among those with ASPD. They may struggle with sustaining long-term relationships and maintaining stable employment.

If you're familiar with the term "drama queen," you already have a basic understanding of HPD. People with this disorder engage in attention-seeking behavior and need constant validation. They exhibit theatrical expressions of emotions and have a strong desire to be the center of attention. Their exaggerated and pretentious behavior can poison relationships, and their need for constant reassurance and admiration may be overwhelming to others.

Cluster C (anxious or fearful thoughts and behaviors) consists of avoidant personality disorder (AVPD), dependent personality disorder (DPD), and obsessive-compulsive personality disorder (OCPD). Individuals with these disorders find it difficult to relax or be at peace. Their worries and controlling natures can be easily triggered.

An intense fear of rejection and avoidance of social situations and relationships characterizes AVPD. Sufferers feel inadequate and are hypersensitive to criticism or disapproval. They tend to isolate themselves while craving acceptance. However, their fears and insecurities hinder their ability to form meaningful connections.

DPD manifests as an excessive need to be taken care of by others. Individuals with DPD have an abnormal fear of separation and often rely on others to make decisions for them. They struggle with assertiveness and have difficulty initiating or maintaining relationships without constant support and reassurance.

If you've ever heard someone referred to as "anal-retentive," the person being described probably exhibits some or all of the symptoms of OCPD. (Anal-retentive refers to Freud's theory that a stressful toilet training experience as a toddler translates into a stuffy, picky, and hyper-vigilant adult.) OCPD is characterized by obsession with perfectionism, orderliness, and control. People with this disorder have rigid thinking patterns, an inflexible attitude toward following rules, and an excessive focus on details. They have difficulty delegating tasks and take a micromanaging approach toward work and productivity. Their perfectionism and inflexibility strain relationships.

Sometimes people manifest a few of the characteristics necessary for a personality disorder but fall short of a full diagnosis. For example, borderline personality disorder can only be diagnosed if the patient meets five or more of nine criteria. But what about people who exhibit only three or four of those symptoms? Diagnostically, they're not borderlines, but they can still engage in BPD-like behavior.

The First Law of Dipsh*ttery states that there is within each of us a dipsh*t yearning to break free. By no means is a mental disorder required. None of us is completely free of psychological "baggage," so we all carry the burden of managing our personal demons and keeping our inner dipsh*t confined.

Substance Abuse and Addiction

Did you happen to notice that there's no mention of any addiction disorder in Clusters A, B, or C? Substance use disorder (SUD) as it's called in the DSM-5 is classified separately. SUD is evaluated on a continuum ranging from mild to severe. Consider the case of Jose Luis Vargas, age 41, a California man described by the San Bernadino County District Attorney's Office as a "habitual drunk driver."

In May of 2023 prosecutors charged that an intoxicated Vargas crashed head-on into a Prius driven by 36-year-old Lisette Villasenor. Her children, Daniel, 6, and Ashley, 12, were passengers. Vargas was not injured in the collision, but Villasenor died and her children were both injured. Young Daniel suffered brain injuries and paralysis. Both survivors will be scarred with the memory of witnessing their mother's violent death.

At the time of the collision, Vargas was on probation for driving under the influence (DUI) in Orange County in 2022. He has prior convictions for drunk driving in Los Angeles, San Diego, and San Bernadino counties. In 2019 he received an official warning that, given his history, any future DUI incident resulting in death could trigger murder charges. And yet Vargas allegedly continued to drink and drive – while on probation for drunk driving. Making good on the state's promise, the district attorney has indicted Vargas for murder and charges related to the children's injuries.

Whether Vargas meets the clinical criteria for a diagnosis of SUD is uncertain. But if the charges against him are true, probability points in that direction. It doesn't require much imagination to see the link between substance abuse, addiction, and reckless, reprehensible behavior. Perhaps the pending criminal charges will mean "last call" for Vargas.

Dipsh*t analytics for this demolition demon:

- **Behavior:** chronic
- **Situation:** frenetic (The situation was not provocative or chaotic until he made it so. But he was driving – a potentially frenetic activity even when sober – so that's what I'll assume.)
- **Cause:** habitual (Certainly, his drinking was a self-induced activity as was his decision to drive while intoxicated. But his serial DUI convictions indicate this was habitual behavior for Vargas.)
- **Outcome:** 5 (destructive) for Villasenor and her children; 5 (destructive) for Vargas, since he now faces catastrophic,

life-altering consequences; 2 (imposing) for first responders, the police and criminal justice system; 3 (disruptive)
for extended family and social services who must now care
for the surviving children.

Impulse Control Disorders

In chapter one you read about Amari Bente Hendricks, the Florida woman who reportedly pulled a gun in a McDonald's drive-
thru because they refused to give her a free cookie. There are any
number of reasons (none of them good) why she might have done
that. Perhaps she was having an extraordinarily bad day. Maybe
she felt the restaurant owed her something because of a problem
with a previous order. She might have had a fight with her significant other and this, combined with immaturity, could have
prompted her behavior. But this is speculation, because we don't
know. There is another possibility, however: Amari could be
struggling with an impulse control disorder. Her extreme overreaction serves as a vivid example of what intermittent explosive disorder (IED) looks like.

IED consists of recurrent episodes of impulsive aggression,
whether verbal or physical, that are disproportionate to the provocation. Other impulse control disorders included in the DSM-5
are kleptomania (stealing), pyromania (setting fires), compulsive
gambling, trichotillomania (pulling out hair), and excoriation
(picking at skin). Each of these diagnoses requires a repetitive history of the damaging and impulsive behavior.

When we learn that someone has been caught shoplifting, we
might conclude that the person is foolish and that such behavior

is deplorable. But suppose the person meets the criteria for a kleptomania diagnosis. We might then empathize with their struggle. However, their disorder does not lessen their responsibility to refrain from stealing, nor does it make shoplifting any less a crime. That's why it's beneficial to know something about psychological disorders and why having a disorder does not automatically excuse disruptive behavior.

Mood Disorders

"Mood" in psychology refers to an emotional state, such as happiness, boredom, anxiety, or worry. A mood disorder is defined by the American Psychological Association as "a prolonged, pervasive emotional disturbance." Major mood disorders identified in the DSM-5 include major depressive disorder (MDD), persistent depressive disorder (PDD), bipolar disorder (types I and II), cyclothymic disorder, and substance/medication-induced bipolar and related disorder.

MDD consists of one or more episodes of depression that last two weeks or more, while PDD is a chronic depressive condition that persists for at least two years in adults and one year in children and adolescents. Bipolar I and II are differentiated by the level and frequency of manic and depressive episodes. Similar to bipolar, cyclothymic disorder involves mood swings, but these are less severe. A diagnosis of substance/medication-induced bipolar is appropriate when mood swings are determined to be directly caused by prescription or illegal drugs.

For a striking example of how undiagnosed bipolar disorder can stimulate outrageous behavior, read about the experience of

Rosie Viva, age 22, a fashion model. In 2018 she experienced a period of hyper-energized mania and didn't sleep. On a day that she planned to fly from London to Croatia, Viva "kissed a stranger in a cafe, stole from shops, and bought everyone breakfast in McDonald's," according to the BBC. At Stansted Airport, she dashed through the baggage drop-off opening and set off a fire alarm. This caused a full-scale evacuation.

Viva stated that she sought medical attention several times but was unable to articulate her symptoms. As a result, her disorder went untreated. After the Stansted incident, however, she was admitted to a psychiatric facility and diagnosed with bipolar I. Viva decided to speak out about her condition and the experiences leading up to her diagnosis as a way of advocating for mental health treatment. *Viva*, Viva!

Because her bipolar disorder was undiagnosed and untreated at the time of her airport misadventure, I will not apply the dipsh*t label to Rosie Viva. If she had known about her bipolar I disorder and didn't take her medication or follow treatment advice, then she would qualify. But it is unethical and unfair to blame someone for bad behavior when that person lacked the cognitive ability to understand the consequences of his or her behavior.

Paraphilias

A man staying at a hotel in Nashville, Tennessee awoke one night to find a stranger sucking on his toes. Daniel Patrick Neal, age 52, a manager at the hotel, reportedly let himself into the male guest's room and applied his tongue to the victim's feet. Neal was charged with aggravated burglary and assault.

Paraphilias consist of abnormal erotic acts or fantasies (such as Neal's alleged foot fetish) that an individual indulges in to achieve sexual gratification. Voyeurism, exhibitionism, sadomasochism, frotteurism (groping), and pedophilia are among the most common paraphilias.

Psychoses

Andrea Yates is a Texas mother who drowned her five children in a bathtub to save them from Satan and send their souls to heaven. Yates was found guilty based on psychiatric testimony that she understood killing one's children to be a crime. In fact, Yates phoned the police after the murders and turned herself in. The legal standard in Texas is whether she understood right from wrong, not whether she was profoundly mentally ill (which she was).

A lesser-known fact about Andrea Yates is that she tried to commit suicide at least twice to prevent herself from killing the children. She was hospitalized several times because of her postpartum depression and psychosis. Physicians prescribed anti-depressants and anti-psychotics, but the latter were discontinued because of side effects. Meanwhile, she and her husband continued having children against doctors' advice.

Phillip J. Resnick, M.D., professor of psychiatry at Case Western Reserver University School of Medicine, provided the following additional context:

In the five weeks between Mrs. Yates's hospital discharge on May 14, 2001 and the drowning of her five children on June 20, 2001, Mrs. Yates had a number of psychotic symptoms. She thought that television commercials for candy were referring directly to her. She believed that one commercial was saying that she was a "fat pig" and that she gave her children too much candy. She had a delusional belief…that television cameras were placed throughout her home to monitor the quality of her mothering. She thought that her mother-in-law was part of the monitoring and that there was a camera in her mother-in-law's glasses. Mrs. Yates also had paranoid ideas that her house was "bugged" because she saw a van near her home. Finally, she had the belief that the one and only Satan was literally within her.

Psychosis is a condition in which a person's thinking and perception have become so distorted that he or she loses touch with reality. This is sometimes called a "psychotic break." Yates' postpartum depression had escalated into full-blown psychosis. That she was profoundly delusional and yet knew killing her children was wrong (though necessary in her view) underscores the tragedy and complexity of this case.

The DSM-5 recognizes schizophrenia spectrum disorders, schizoaffective disorder, delusional disorder, brief psychotic disorder, and schizophreniform disorder as psychoses. Schizophrenia is the "poster child" of psychotic disorders. It's a profound and chronic distortion of mental functioning, which can include delusions, hallucinations, disorganized thoughts and speech, catatonia, and self-neglect. Schizoaffective disorder includes symptoms of schizophrenia combined with those of mood disorders, such as major depressive episodes or manic episodes.

Delusional disorder is diagnosed when a person experiences chronic, non-bizarre delusions. A "non-bizarre" delusion is a belief that is demonstrably false yet within the realm of possibility. For example, if I believed that I have visited every country in Africa when I have not, that would be a non-bizarre delusion. But if I believed that I have visited every planet in the solar system, that would be a bizarre delusion.

A brief psychotic disorder, as the name implies, is a temporary condition lasting at least one day but less than a month. Symptoms may include hallucinations, delusions, disorganized speech, or grossly disorganized or catatonic behavior. This diagnosis is only appropriate when the patient returns to a pre-psychotic state of normality within a month.

Schizophreniform disorder is essentially temporary schizophrenia. This diagnosis is appropriate if symptoms last at least a month but less than six months. If the condition persists after six months, then it qualifies as schizophrenia.

Now consider the case of 33-year-old Kieran Hayes, a paranoid schizophrenic in the United Kingdom who attacked and drowned a fisherman. According to *The Mirror*, "Hayes began to hallucinate that [the victim] was another person who he wrongly believed had assaulted his mother." Kevin Hodkinson, age 50, was found dead in Oxspring Dam, a private pond in Sheffield, South Yorkshire. Hayes' strange behavior in the vicinity, including running barefoot past the crime scene, aroused suspicions and led to his arrest. A court accepted a guilty plea to manslaughter in lieu of murder and committed Hayes indefinitely to a psychiatric hospital.

As with the Andrea Yates murders, the Hayes homicide was shocking and senseless, affecting both the victim and his surviving family members. Both Yates and Hayes are confined indefinitely, the former in prison and the latter in a mental hospital. Yates knew she was violating the law, but in her addled state believed she was answering to a higher morality and "saving" her children's souls. Hayes thought he was punishing someone who he believed had attacked his mother.

Ordinarily, murders that are intentional and without any justification would qualify as dipsh*ttery (to say the least). And yet Yates and Hayes do not deserve vilification. Their crimes are horrific. The fact that they were psychotic does not change that. But because of their psychosis, we should recognize that they were profoundly impaired and out of touch with reality when they killed. So we shouldn't further stigmatize them.

When Our Brains "Phone It In"

We all have *heuristics* and *schemas* that help us to get by in the world. A heuristic is a handy rule or habit that allows us to function without having to ponder every minute detail of daily life. For example, "look both ways" is a heuristic that allows us to cross the street without conducting a detailed analysis of risks and logistics. Other familiar heuristics are "checked that it's plugged in" when an electric appliance doesn't work and "give it some gas" when your car won't start on the first try.

A schema is similar to a heuristic but paints a bigger picture. It's a mental framework or model that helps us understand people, things, and situations without laborious cognitive effort. For example, when we think of "shoes," we instantly understand that they come as a pair, that one shoe will go on the right foot, one shoe will go on the left foot, and that they must be size-appropriate, because one size does not fit all. When you think of "job interview," you know approximately what kind of dress is appropriate, how everyone involved will be expected to act (as opposed to their behavior at a pub, for example), and the kinds of questions you should be prepared to answer.

Now imagine what can go wrong when our heuristics are either inappropriate or too simplistic for a particular situation. And consider the possible consequences when we apply an incorrect or inadequate schema to the wrong person, place, or thing. The following examples will illustrate.

Shortly after midnight four high school cheerleaders arrived at a supermarket parking lot in Texas after returning from an out-of-town practice. They used the parking lot as a carpool rendezvous point. Heather Roth approached a car that looked like her rideshare and opened the door, only to see a strange man inside. Realizing her mistake, Roth quickly closed the door and returned to her previous vehicle.

Roth said the man then got out of his vehicle and followed her to the car containing the cheerleaders. She rolled down her window to apologize, but the man pulled a gun and began firing. He struck Roth and one other girl. A witness said he saw 25-year-old Pedro Tello Rodriguez, Jr. fire several shots at the cheerleaders' car and then flee. Both girls survived.

Rodriguez is charged with third-degree "deadly conduct."

In this case, Roth's schema (the make, model, and color of her carpool vehicle) proved inadequate because it wasn't specific enough to distinguish the correct car from look-alikes. Roth's mistake could happen to any of us. I once got into the wrong car at a commuter train station. I was expecting my wife to pick me up, and the car I got into looked just like hers. Sometimes our schemas need a few additional details, a fact we only discover when we make such mistakes.

Rodriguez (the dipsh*t in this example) also relied on a schema that was unsuited for this situation. The supermarket parking lot presumably was sparsely populated because of the late hour. Naturally, he would be startled if a stranger opened his car door. This being Texas, he might have gotten away with shooting her if he had fired mere seconds after she opened his door. But Roth quickly closed the door and returned to her vehicle. Rodriguez got out and pursued her. He then opened fire on a vehicle occupied by four people. His Texas-themed self-defense schema turned out to be an irresponsible and destructive behavioral model in this situation.

Dipsh*t analytics for Quick-Draw Rodriguez:

- **Behavior:** chronic (When in doubt...)
- **Situation:** provocative (Roth provoked Rodriguez when she opened his door. But the situation would have quickly returned to normal if Rodriquez had used a bit of common sense. Clearly, any danger had passed by the time he fired his gun.)
- **Cause:** triggered (Rodriguez over-reacted in response to Roth's mistake.)

- **Outcome:** 5 (destructive) for the girls who were shot (one critically injured) and their families; 4 (damaging) for the non-injured girls who witnessed the shooting; 2 (imposing) for first responders, the police and criminal justice system; 4 or 5 (damaging or destructive) for Rodriguez if he is convicted, depending on the level of punishment.

Groups need heuristics and schemas just as people do. Families, organizations, governments, and even international alliances can benefit from these mental shortcuts. And just like people, they can experience blowback when their simplistic solutions prove to be misguided. Consider the infamous Munich Agreement negotiated by Neville Chamberlain with Adolf Hitler. The Fuhrer threatened war unless Czechoslovakia ceded a portion of its territory known as the Sudetenland to Germany. That region was occupied mostly by ethnic Germans. To avoid a second world war in Europe, Chamberlain brokered a peace deal in which the major European powers would accede to Hitler's annexation of the Sudetenland in exchange for Hitler's promise to forego any further territorial demands or threats of war.

As Europe soon learned, Hitler had no intention of honoring this peace treaty. Germany invaded Poland, whereupon England and France declared war. Chamberlain discovered to his dismay that the schema of "negotiated peace treaties" based on honor among heads of state meant nothing when one of the parties was a genocidal dictator.

For an example of a failed heuristic, consider the experience of Proctor and Gamble when they introduced disposable diapers in Japan. At the time, Pampers in the United States were sold in packaging with an image of a stork carrying a bundle of Pampers. That's a heuristic representing a newborn infant, and it's a familiar symbol to people in the U.S. At the time, however, the concept of storks delivering babies was unfamiliar to the Japanese. They didn't understand the meaning of this strange bird on diaper packages.

Heuristics frequently fail to transfer seamlessly from one culture to another. In the United States and other Western countries, a "thumb-up" gesture means "OK." But you'd be asking for trouble if you flashed your thumb in the Middle East or West Africa. To people there it means "up yours!" Failing to recognize and respect social norms when visiting other countries can peg you as a denizen of Dipsh*tville.

Dipsh*t Destructiveness Writ Large

Before I retired from higher education, I worked at a Catholic university in New Orleans. The school had a nursing program and wanted to expand its offerings by starting a physician assistant (PA) program. The president, who had a history of making questionable decisions, hired an out-of-state PA, "Mr. Love," as program director.

At first, Mr. Love, age 64, was the only person working in the fledgling PA program. The school had neither the qualified personnel nor sufficient medical equipment to begin enrolling students. Mr. Love was tasked with planning the new PA program from scratch and acquiring whatever assets would be needed to make it a reality. He generated much activity with planning sessions and lots of talk (boy oh boy, could he talk), but weeks passed with little to show for his efforts.

The vice president of academic affairs asked me to advise Mr. Love on getting grants for some of the necessary equipment, since I have won many government grants and contracts. But I could make little headway with him. When we had our grant meeting, he talked incessantly about himself and his purported history of treating high-level government officials in Washington, D.C. I found him to be both superficial and grandiose.

A few weeks later, local media reported the shocking news that Mr. Love had been arrested for molesting a boy repeatedly from 1998 to 2001. Incredibly, this pederast had reached out to his victim on Facebook and admitted his guilt during a live chat. The victim made a recording and turned it over to police. Mr. Love waived extradition to Maine, where the crimes occurred. At least one other victim came forward afterwards. It was also revealed that he had once been a Scoutmaster, and some suspicious activity with boys may have occurred then as well.

Today Mr. Love is serving a 7-year sentence to be followed by 12 years' probation. In the wake of this debacle, the university abandoned plans for a PA program. And the icing on this rancid cake is this: Mr. Love had never even bothered to obtain licensure as a PA in Louisiana. Apparently, the university president, who personally recruited this bozo, never bothered to check.

Here are the dipsh*t analytics for this medical molester:

- **Behavior:** chronic (I was tempted to classify him as "hybrid," since molestation is only one aspect of his seemingly normal life. But when I recalled how ineffective he was at launching the PA program, I had to go with "chronic.")

- **Situation:** benign
- **Cause:** habitual
- **Outcome:** 5 (destructive) for Mr. Love's victims and their families; 5 (destructive) for Mr. Love himself; 4 (damaging) for the university; 2 (imposing) for the police, prosecutor, and court.
- Using the four-factor model of foolishness, Cipolla's laws of human stupidity, and dipsh*t analytics, how would you rate Mr. Love's behavior during the time he was molesting kids? During his short, useless tenure as PA program director? When he reconnected with his victim via Facebook and confessed his crimes?

* * *

"We have met the enemy, and he is us."
 – Pogo the 'Possum

Chapter Four

The Third Law: Although Sometimes Unavoidable, it is Always a Mistake to Interact with Dipsh*ts

In April 2023 Tanner Cook and two accomplices entered the food court at Dulles Town Center, a mall in Virginia. The trio are YouTube so-called pranksters who harass and annoy strangers and then post videos of their angry, frustrated, or confused victims to their channel, "Classified Goons." Some of their previous stunts resulted in police responding to the scene. Cook in particular was well-known to the mall's security guards and to local cops, so he had to be wary of detection.

As his two helpers recorded the incident, Cook approached, Alan Colie, 31, and began shoving his cell phone at the man. Cook later testified at a court hearing that the phone was playing a nonsense message, "Hey dipsh*t, stop thinking about my sparkle." He reportedly kept advancing on Colie even as the man told him to stop and motioned him away. At one point Cook allegedly held his phone a mere six inches (15 cm) from Colie's face.

Finally, Colie drew a pistol and shot his tormentor point-blank. Cook survived, but the bullet ruptured his liver. Colie was arrested and remains in jail waiting for a grand jury to decide whether the shooting was justifiable self-defense.

According to NBC News, Cook's father "said his son is 'a good kid that doesn't have a mean bone in his body.' He added that Tanner wants to provide entertainment to people." Apparently Alan Colie and many others targeted by these three miscreants didn't appreciate being cast as unwilling participants in this exploitative type of "entertainment."

Dipsh*t analytics for Cook and his compatriots:

- **Behavior:** chronic
- **Situation:** benign (Only their misconduct made the situation tense.)
- **Cause:** self-induced
- **Outcome:** 5 (destructive) for their victim, who sits in jail; 4 (damaging) for Cook and his family; 3 (disruptive) for witnesses and mall personnel; (2) imposing for the police, prosecutor, grand jury, and court.

Dipsh*t analytics for Alan Colie, whose decision to shoot in reaction to this obnoxious provocation strikes me as a disproportionate use of force. He was harassed but not in immediate danger. The situation could have been resolved without gunfire.

- **Behavior:** occasional (I think he deserves the benefit of the doubt.)
- **Situation:** provocative
- **Cause:** triggered (No pun intended.)
- **Outcome:** 5 (destructive) for Colie, since he's in jail and awaiting a grand jury's decision; 4 (damaging) for Cook

and his family; 3 (disruptive) for witnesses and mall personnel; (2) imposing for the police, prosecutor, grand jury, and court.

What Were They Thinking?

When is a prank not a prank? Perhaps it ceases to qualify as such when someone pulls a gun, or when police respond to the scene, or when a life-threatening injury is inflicted. Cook and his friends' attempts to pass off their social media intrusions as "pranks" don't pass the smell test. That would be like calling Cook's gunshot wound a "boo-boo." The description minimizes what happened and omits many essential details.

A prank is an annoying but harmless trick played on someone. Accosting strangers in a threatening, intimidating, or aggressive manner is not a prank. Any confrontation that could result in foreseeable violence or even death is not a prank. Such outrageous and despicable provocations are malicious mischief.

Another YouTuber wasn't as lucky as Tanner Cook. On a fateful night in Nashville, Tennessee, Timothy Wilks, 20, and an unnamed friend armed themselves with butcher knives. They intended to fake a robbery and record it for social media. This pair of Darwin Award contenders menaced a group of people in a parking lot as they were leaving a "trampoline park." David Starnes, Jr., who did not realize that this was a social media stunt, drew his pistol and killed Wilks. Starnes was not charged. Dipsh*t analytics for Wilks and his friend would be the same as for Tanner Cook and his accomplices.

The random strangers who were targeted by these YouTube hooligans didn't willingly participate in the stunts. Their involuntary involvement shows that we must sometimes deal with stupid and vexatious people even against our will. Nevertheless, getting involved with them usually turns out to be a painful experience. You might be wondering why these young men thought they could hijack public places and private businesses as venues for their mayhem. And didn't they realize that sooner or later these stunts would turn ugly if they continued harassing people? Certainly, they were young, immature, and reckless. But by the age of 20, most of us know that we can't provoke strangers without risking retaliation. Either they didn't care or they were so intoxicated by social media fame that they lost all perspective. We don't know anything about their home environments or life experiences, but it's not unreasonable to suspect that these may have been contributing influences. However, let's dig deeper and examine their noxious behavior in light of sociological and psychological theories.

In his book, *Thinking, Fast and Slow*, psychologist Daniel Kahneman popularized the concept of *System 1* (fast) and *System 2* (slow) thinking. Briefly, thinking that's automatic, emotional, and reactionary, including your fight-or-flight instinct, makes up System 1. Driving a car while letting your mind wander or tying your shoes without consciously focusing on your finger movements are examples of System 1 in action.

System 2 thinking occurs when you concentrate. These thoughts are cautious, deliberative, and rational. You engage System 2 when you prepare your tax return or learn how to use a new software program. Kahneman didn't originate the concept of fast and slow thinking, but his book helped make these concepts widely known and understood.

System 1 thoughts make up most of our mental activity. Heuristics and schemas, the mental shortcuts discussed in chapter 3, are forms of fast thinking. System 2 is dependent on System 1 in that our emotional, reactive, fast-thinking mind feeds snap judgments and emotional impulses to System 2 for consideration. Our slow-thinking mind can then provide rational justifications for transforming our passions into convictions and beliefs. On the other hand, it's also true that our logical, higher-order mind can govern our irrational urges and restrain the knee-jerk reactions of System 1. The YouTubers who accost strangers in pursuit of social media likes seem to be letting their System 1 thinking run riot, without any System 2 override.

A useful theory for understanding how behaviors, attitudes, and emotions spread through social networks is *social contagion theory*. People are susceptible to "catching" behaviors and ideas from others, leading to a ripple effect that influences group dynamics. An interesting example of this is an incident known as "the great June bug epidemic." In 1962, a group of women working in a factory came to believe that they had been bitten by a bug. One woman (the "carrier") began displaying symptoms of illness and blamed her condition on a bug bite. One by one, the others began manifesting symptoms and claiming that they too had been bitten. No bug was ever found, and doctors discovered no cause for their symptoms. The entire episode was attributed to mass psychosis.

As we know, the Internet has made "going viral" possible instantaneously. This interconnectedness, combined with the addictive properties of social media fame, can cause the phenomenon of social contagion to spiral out of control. Young people in particular are lured by the appeal of widespread popularity, thousands of "likes," and easy money. They see others building a fan base as "influencers," and want in on the excitement. Without healthy System 2 regulation of their impulses, their conduct can exceed reasonable behavioral boundaries.

Consider for example dangerous and sometimes deadly TikTok challenges. A social media "influencer" in China, Wang Moufeng, age 34, participated in a challenge by downing four bottles of baijiu, also known as Chinese vodka. The beverage has an alcohol content of up to 60 percent. Hours later, Wang was dead of alcohol poisoning. Mason Dark, a high school student in North Carolina, fared much better with his TikTok challenge – he sustained burns over 76 percent of his body, but survived. He and some friends decided to emulate videos of people fooling around with fire and spray paint cans. A can exploded and rained fire on the hapless teen.

At his age, Wang (may he rest in peace) should have known better. But as mentioned in chapter one, kids and teenagers deserve to be cut some slack. I suspect Mason has learned a thing or two about dares, peer pressure, and risky behavior.

From the opioid epidemic to the proliferation of mass shootings to the rise of extremist political movements, the results of social contagion cannot escape notice. And while the U.S. seemingly produces more dipsh*ts per capita that other nations, there are strong contenders elsewhere in the world. Germany, for example, has its own insurrectionists willing to overthrow the government.

In December 2022 authorities arrested 25 members of a far-right extremist group for planning a coup d'état. Patriotische Union ("Patriotic Union"), reportedly known for violence and antisemitism, wanted to establish a non-democratic government with a supreme leader. (Haven't we seen this movie before?) Apparently these dipsh*ts intended to add a distinctly 21st century twist to authoritarianism, because they embraced QAnon and COVID-19 denial.

Dipsh*t analytics for these Teutonic terrorists:

- **Behavior:** chronic
- **Situation:** frenetic (I don't know anything about the German political climate, but in my experience politics in general tend to be frenetic, or worse.)
- **Cause:** habitual (Confirmed malcontents.)
- **Outcome:** 5 (destructive) for those arrested, especially if convicted and punished; 3 (disruptive) for the German government, which had to deploy large numbers of police and military officers to investigate the plot; 2 (imposing) for justice system that will have to prosecute the accused and punish them if convicted.

Fleecing the Flock

If the malicious hijinks of young people seeking social media fame seem reckless, just compare them to mature, yet stupefyingly boneheaded, adults. Using the pretext of religion to sell bogus medical remedies would certainly signal that one is dabbling in dipsh*ttery. But that's exactly what some charlatans did at the height of the pandemic.

Today we might chuckle at the gullibility of 19th and early 20th century people who put their trust in "snake oil" remedies. Potions such as "Kickapoo Indian Sagwa" promised to cure "constipation, liver complaint, dyspepsia, indigestion, loss of appetite, scrofula, rheumatism, chills, fever, or any disease." Even Coca-Cola was originally promoted as a remedy for morphine addiction, digestive problems, nervous conditions, impotence, and headaches.

Most people at that time lived on farms or in small towns and never traveled more than a few miles from their homes. There were few laws to protect people from patent remedy hucksters and no government agencies to test and approve effective medicines. Medical science was still primitive by today's standards. Even family doctors may have trusted and prescribed these dubious drugs.

Fast-forward to the 21st century, and what are we to make of people who purchased a bogus COVID-19 "cure" at the height of the pandemic from an equally bogus "church" in Florida? Mark Grenon, age 62, and his three adult sons founded the "Genesis II Church of Health and Healing" under the assumption that a veneer of religion would insulate them from prosecution. They then began selling "Miracle Mineral Solution," a mixture of sodium chlorite and water which metabolizes into chlorine dioxide in the body. Drinking the Grenons' concoction would be essentially the same as drinking bleach and could cause serious injury or death.

The Genesis II church itself was a legal fiction. According to the U.S. Justice Department, Mark Grenon admitted that it "has nothing to do with religion," and that he founded Genesis to "legalize the use of MMS" and avoid "going to jail." And just to double-down on their criminality, the Grenons violated court orders by continuing to sell their dangerous elixir even after the government obtained injunctions requiring them to cease and desist.

When the Justice Department finally indicted them, at least two of the Grenons fled to Colombia. All were eventually apprehended, and Mark Grenon was extradited to the U.S. to face trial.

But surely customers for the Grenons' toxic concoction were few in number, right? After all, people get cures for deadly diseases from healthcare professionals, pharmacies, or hospitals, not churches. Surely a weird religion claiming to have the only remedy for a worldwide pandemic would evoke skepticism in all but the most gullible people. Unfortunately, the sheer abundance of dipsh*t customers made Miracle Mineral Solution a financial success. Prosecutors estimate that about $1 million worth of the poison was sold.

That the Grenons were hucksters selling a bogus product should have been apparent to anyone with a modicum of common sense. Not only did they claim that their glorified bleach could cure COVID-19, they also promoted it as a panacea for "cancer, Alzheimer's, diabetes, autism, malaria, hepatitis, Parkinson's, herpes, HIV/AIDS, and other serious medical conditions," according to the Justice Department. Yet many people believed these fantastical claims and trusted their health to this unproven (and ultimately hazardous) potion.

We can't always avoid dealing with dipsh*ts no matter how much we might want to, as the obnoxious YouTubers who accost strangers demonstrate. But we can certainly avoid those like the Grenons whose actions flash a warning if we simply pay attention. It's bad enough to get entangled with dipsh*ts against our will. But it's quite another to plunge headlong into foreseeable abuse, as buyers of Miracle Mineral Solution did.

Dipsh*t analytics for Mark Grenon and sons, alias the "bleach boys":

- **Behavior:** chronic
- **Situation:** provocative (a deadly pandemic had thrown the world into chaos)
- **Cause:** habitual (Their defiance of court orders and flight to avoid prosecution shows them to be constant dipsh*ts.)
- **Outcome:** 5 (destructive) for the Grenons; 4 or 5 (damaging or destructive) for any customers who were injured or killed by their toxic sludge; 2 (imposing) for the authorities and justice system who had to sue, prosecute, and ultimately extradite these cretins.

There were so many customers conned by the Grenons that a one-size-fits-all dipsh*t analysis for the "typical" customer is elusive. Some may have been gravely ill with COVID-19 and desperate for any chance of survival. Others may have been healthy but exceptionally fearful. A fair number were probably just gullible. I'll take the most generous view possible.

- **Behavior:** occasional (I'm attributing customers' behavior to sickness or fear.)

- **Situation:** provocative
- **Cause:** triggered
- **Outcome:** 4 or 5 (damaging or destructive) for anyone injured or killed by this "miracle" product and for their families as well; 2 (imposing) for those who were scammed but not injured.

The Grenons weren't the only ecclesiastical con men hawking pseudo-remedies during the pandemic. Bishop Climate Wiseman, age 47, of the Kingdom Church in Camberwell, south London, was convicted of fraud for selling "plague protection oil" for £91. Wiseman told his parishioners that they could "end up dropping dead" if they didn't buy his miracle tonic. Likewise, televangelist and convicted felon, Jim Bakker, used the veneer of religion to promote "Silver Solution" as a preventative or cure for COVID-19. Not only were the claims unsubstantiated, but regulators warned that high concentrations of silver can cause the skin to turn blue. The attorney general of Missouri, where Bakker's ministry is based, sued. Bakker was forced pay $156,000 in restitution.

The Attachment Angle

Social control theory, developed by sociologist Travis Hirschi in the 1960s, seeks to explain people's motivation to conform to society's expectations, and why they sometimes don't. According to Hirschi's model, four factors influence our willingness or unwillingness to behave as good friends, neighbors, and citizens. These are *attachment, commitment, involvement*, and *belief.*

The attachment element consists of strong bonds (or lack thereof) with friends, family, and community. A young man in the United States, for example, is less likely to be tempted to commit crimes if he maintains close bonds with his family, develops the right kinds of friendships, and feels connected to this community through work, school, church, or volunteerism. As globalization, political polarization, the pandemic, economic uncertainty, and other macrotrends have eroded social connectedness, we have seen a rise in social unrest, public aggression and violence, and the kind of spiteful divisiveness that tears at the fabric of civilized society.

Commitment to the traditional goals of education, career, family, religious participation, and good citizenship also serve as predictors of social stability. Shifting demographics, politics, and attitudes toward traditional social roles can cause individuals to feel disconnected. As old values and institutions undergo change, people may feel that their society and culture lacks relevance or permanence.

If an individual's attachment or commitment is weak, then he or she isn't likely to maintain a healthy level of involvement. Teens not involved in sports, church, or other pro-social activities risk getting into mischief. Adults without stable employment and relationships will probably feel less invested in society. And so we see the cumulative effect of attachment, commitment, and involvement as strengthening social assimilation, while the absence of these intangibles amounts to a lack of restraint on misconduct.

Finally, the belief element of social control theory holds that a person is more likely to fit in and act as a responsible member of society when he or she has faith in the moral validity of social customs, norms, and institutions. Ironically, it's people with strong bonds and beliefs that leave themselves open for victimization by a specific type of chicanery– namely, *affinity fraud.*

People who bought bogus COVID-19 cures from televangelist Jim Bakker or Bishop Climate Wiseman were probably duped because they trusted these ministers and did not expect prominent fellow Christians to scam them. Affinity fraud is deception based on exploitation of trust within a close-knit group. Any collection of people with common bonds – coworkers, alumni, gangs, civic clubs, or fraternities, for example – can be fertile ground for interpersonal exploitation. Many victims of Bernard Madoff's pyramid scheme were fellow Jews referred to him by word of mouth within that community.

Gullibility and Greed

Before I retired from higher education, I taught both business and psychology courses (I have graduate degrees in both fields). Occasionally business students would drop by my office for advice about some investment opportunity or entrepreneurial idea. One day a young man came to show me a money-making scheme he'd gotten involved with.

This student had signed up to be an "independent distributor" for a multi-level marketing (MLM) corporation. The company sold memberships in a discount travel club. As he presented me with marketing brochures and began to describe the vast wealth soon to be his, I asked him to wait a moment while I Googled the company.

First, I checked their rating with the Better Business Bureau, which I expected to be mediocre at best. In fact, they had a "D" rating on a scale of A+ to F. When I pointed this out to the student, he dismissed it as unimportant. Next, I called his attention to page after page of negative reviews from customers and former distributors. In what can only be described as a breathtakingly clueless response, he launched into a hard-sell pitch to recruit me into the company (because he would earn a commission on the sales of anyone he recruited).

I quickly cut him off and ushered him out of my office. I was fresh out of patience with his willful blindness. A couple of weeks later, he dropped out of college to devote full-time to this MLM.

It's bad enough when unavoidable circumstances force us to deal with dipsh*ts. But to volunteer for disaster by failing to heed obvious red flags, as my student did with this MLM, is itself a dipsh*t move. And the MLM industry, regardless of the company, is its own red flag.

College campuses have become fertile recruiting grounds for these schemes. Students typically lack the knowledge and experience to recognize MLMs as traps for the unwary. And being perpetually short of cash, they're understandably attracted to side hustles that seem legitimate and lucrative.

In an article addressing the exploitation of students by MLMs, William W. Keep, Ph.D., professor of marketing and interdisciplinary business at The College of New Jersey wrote,

> The potential for damage due to exaggerated MLM income claims was illustrated by a parent who described in an email to me what had happened to her son: 'Not only did [my son] drop out of college, but he has been living on the streets in his car for

the past three weeks. My son has been persuaded by Vemma's training and negative influences to have unrealistic expectations for earning an income.'

The Internet is awash with tragic stories of people who joined MLMs to their physical, emotional, and financial detriment. These get-rich "opportunities" are promoted with false promises of unlimited wealth, financial independence, freedom from dead-end jobs, and the prestige of owning one's own business. In fact, the typical MLM distributor works innumerable hours; makes few sales of the over-priced products; and alienates friends, family, and strangers by pressuring them to join. Most people recruited into MLMs eventually quit once they see that their time and effort are yielding minimal payoff. According to the Direct Selling Association, the median earnings of MLM distributors across all companies is a mere $2,400 per year.

What would an MLM recruitment pitch look like if worded honestly? Here's an example:

Sign up with our company and become a straight-commission salesperson. We make no guarantee that you'll earn a living wage – or anything at all. Whenever you're not sleeping, you'll be working.

Our over-priced products don't exactly fly off the shelves, so your best chance of earning money is to recruit others. As you pursue new recruits, you'll make a pest of yourself to everyone you know and to strangers as well. What's more, we don't even provide you with products to sell. You'll have to buy your inventory from us in advance.

For a classic example of MLM fraud, consider the case of Success By Health (SBH) and VOZ Travel (VOZ), operated by

James D. "Jay" Noland, Jr., Lina Noland, Scott Harris, and Thomas Sacca. According to the Federal Trade Commission (FTC), a federal court "found that the Nolands, Harris, and Sacca violated the FTC Act by operating SBH and VOZ Travel as pyramid schemes and using false promises of 'financial freedom.'" During a group presentation, Harris allegedly proclaimed, "Is this one of those pyramid things? Hell, yeah it is. If it wasn't, I wouldn't be doing it. Do I look dumb enough to go get a job again?" But wait, there's more!

> In addition, the court ruled that the defendants' false claims about Noland's own wealth in selling the pyramid schemes were "outrageous." Noland, for example, told SBH and VOZ Travel members, "I've been financially free, completely time and money free since I was 36." In fact, as the court found, at the age of 36, Noland "was living (or was about to start living) off credit cards."
>
> Additionally, although Noland told SBH and VOZ members he was a multi-millionaire, the court explained that "[i]n his January 2020 sworn financial statement, Noland reported he had a negative net worth." Similarly, at a deposition in this case, "Noland was unable to identify a time he *ever* had a positive net worth."

How's that for low-down, double-dealing bamboozling? Whenever you encounter an MLM, consider it a warning. And if you're offered "the chance of lifetime" by a member of your church, school, workplace, or other group, consider whether you're a target of affinity fraud.

Dipsh*t analytics for the Nolands, Harris, and Sacca, the miscreants of MLM:

- **Behavior:** chronic

- **Situation:** benign
- **Cause:** self-induced (Can't rule out habitual, but we don't know their history.)
- **Outcome:** 5 (destructive) for the defendants who were slapped with a $7.3 million judgment and banned from operating an MLM (this was a civil case, not criminal); 4 (damaging) for those who invested time and money as distributors; 2 (imposing) for the FTC, prosecutor, and federal court.

Self-Defense: Avoid-Evade-Defend

So far I've applied dipsh*t analytics after the fact to the cases in each chapter, and I'll continue doing so. But you'll be able to protect yourself only if you analyze dipsh*t behavior at the time it occurs. By assessing these obtuse and obnoxious individuals in real time, you'll be able to intelligently apply the skills and strengths from your anti-dipsh*t list to avoiding, evading, or defending against their misdeeds.

In chapter two I recommended that you compile a list of the strengths and skills you can use to keep your inner dipsh*t under control during times when you might be tempted to "let 'er rip." My own list includes patience, sense of humor, empathy, and critical thinking, to name a few. Your list should be reflective of your personality. If you haven't started your anti-dipsh*t list yet, why not do it now? Continue adding to it as you become aware of latent abilities.

Here's how I applied dipsh*t analytics in real time to assess and respond to a problem: A few months ago, I was staying in a hotel room with a balcony that overlooked the parking lot. I could see my car below. I happened to notice that a woman was parking her car directly behind mine, blocking me in. This seemed strange, because there were plenty of empty parking spots and she was parking illegally.

When she got out and walked toward the building, I stepped out onto my balcony and asked her, "Excuse me, but is there some reason you're blocking me in?" Without even looking at me she screamed, "Don't you come out here and start something with me! I will f*** you up!"

Wow. Not quite believing what I'd heard, I said: "It's not a problem if you're just going to be a few minutes." But she was just getting started. "I'll stay as long as I damn please! We don't even want you here!"

I didn't know her, and she didn't know me, so "we" not wanting me here made no sense. I was a registered guest, and the hotel certainly wanted me. But I concluded from this bizarre exchange that she was probably mentally ill – possibly an ambulatory schizophrenic. (Bear in mind our rule: We don't stigmatize profoundly mentally ill people who are incompetent. But people who are functional adults, regardless of their mental challenges, must be held accountable for their actions. This woman was driving and going about her business in the adult world.)

Based on this brief, unpleasant encounter, I was able to conclude...

- **Behavior:** chronic (This is our default rating absent evidence to the contrary.)
- **Situation:** benign

- **Cause:** triggered (By my asking about her parking.)
- **Outcome:** 2 (imposing) for me, and as you'll see, it was 3 (disruptive) for her.

I realized that arguing with her or confronting her would only escalate the conflict and possibly prove dangerous, depending on her emotional state. So I waited about twenty minutes to see if she would return and move her car. When she didn't, I called the front desk and asked to speak with hotel security. Long story short, a security officer blocked *her* car with his vehicle and called a tow truck. When she finally returned, she discovered that I was no longer blocked in – and her vehicle had been towed away.

As a general rule, I recommend the following defensive tactics against dipsh*ts, based on their behavioral type – occasional, chronic, or hybrid. With the occasional type, it's a good idea to try reasoning with them and de-escalating the situation. This can work with those who are usually responsible and receptive to a level-headed approach. With chronic types, you'd be well advised to *avoid, evade, or defend.* (These are similar to the run-hide-fight tactics recommended in response to an active shooter.) For example, with the hotel parking lot woman, I tried to avoid dealing with her by waiting to see if she moved her car in a reasonable time. When she didn't, I went into "defend" mode by summoning hotel security. With the hybrid type, consider a dual approach – reasoning and de-escalation first, but moving quickly to avoid, evade, or defend if necessary.

Notice that responding to dipsh*ttery with your own dipsh*ttery is not a recommended tactic. Alan Colie, the man who allegedly shot YouTuber Tanner Cook, overreacted when his peaceful attempts to end the harassment didn't succeed. Now he sits in jail because he used a gun. Put yourself in his place and consider the strengths and skills on your anti-dipsh*t list. How would you have avoided, evaded, or defended against Cook's antagonism without using deadly force?

We live in an age wherein stupid and despicable people abound. The farce is strong with them. Avoid, evade, or defend must be our Jedi mind tricks.

* * *

"I'm fairly certain that YOLO is *carpe diem* for stupid people."
– Jack Black

Chapter Five

The Fourth Law: When in Doubt, Always Assume
That a Dips*t is the Chronic Type Unless There is
Good Reason to Believe Otherwise

Amsterdam, known as the "city of canals," wants young British
men to kindly stop p*ssing and puking in them. The Dutch city
has launched what the BBC calls "a digital discouragement campaign targeting men aged 18 to 35 in the UK." Their message to
sex- and drug-addled Brits boils down to, "Bugger off!" Notoriously libertine Amsterdam is finally fed up with rowdy hooligans
"urinating in public, throwing up in canals, stripping off and engaging in drunken brawls," the BBC reports.

Cheap flights from Britain to Amsterdam have enabled the de-
bauchery, along with travel agencies promoting "stag weekends in
Amsterdam, including canal boat cruises with unlimited booze,
'steak and strip' nights and red-light district pub crawls," according to the BBC. Now, when members of that unwanted demographic search for such hedonism online, they are confronted with
graphic videos of arrests or of unconscious young men being
loaded into ambulances.

Of course, people from all over the world visit Amsterdam because of its free-wheeling reputation. And more than a few of

them probably get drunk, urinate in the canals, and commit other offenses. For many years I lived in New Orleans and witnessed similar behavior in the French Quarter, especially during Mardi Gras. For the Dutch capital to specifically single out British men suggests that their boorishness is an order of magnitude greater than that of other nations. (But CNN reports that the "Stay Away" campaign may be expanded to additional EU countries in the future.)

Amsterdam's "digital discouragement campaign" epitomizes the fourth law of dipsh*ttery. City leaders have decided – rightly or wrongly – that it's in their interest to assume that young men from the UK are prone to be wankers, rather than remaining passive and accepting the onslaught of bad behavior. Certainly, many British men do not commit offensive acts and would be welcome guests in Amsterdam and elsewhere. But the "Stay Away" campaign presupposes an entire demographic to be dipsh*t-prone.

While Amsterdam's campaign may be an effective defensive measure for the city (and probably came about as a last resort), I think we should be cautious about damning an entire group. For our purposes, I recommend applying the fourth law on a case-by-case basis and not broadly against a population.

Let Me Call You Karen

"Karens" is the 21st century tag for middle-aged white women who vent their rage, retaliation, and faux victimhood in public places as an extreme reaction to trivial provocations (or no provocation at all). They qualify as chronic dipsh*ts. Since all Karens by definition have committed offensive and abusive acts, I'm not excoriating all middle-aged white women – only the guilty. And I offer my regrets to ladies whose actual name is Karen and who don't behave this way.

Though less well-known than their Karen counterparts, let's not forget that middle-aged white men also act out from time to time. They have become known as "Kevins" or "Kens." The chronic label applies to them as well. As with Karens, I intend no offense to well-behaved men named Kevin or Ken.

Working While Black. In Nashville, Tennessee, Bitsy Brennan and her 27-year-old son, Edward, noticed an unfamiliar black man in the parking garage of their apartment building. They took it upon themselves to investigate. This Karen and Kevin duo accosted Johnny Martinez, an African-American, and began questioning him. Martinez took out his phone and began recording as the Brennans approached. Bitsy Brennan said, "You don't belong here. How did you get here?"

Martinez declined to explain himself to this pair of busybodies. He said afterwards that it should have been obvious he was working, because he wore a headlamp, kneepads, and a lanyard. Martinez had been hired to check parking permits in the garage so that illegally parked vehicles could be immobilized (i.e., "booted").

Edward Brennan apparently became vexed that this uppity black man wouldn't submit to interrogation. He screamed, "Get the f*** out of my building," and took a swing at Martinez, narrowly missing his face. Meanwhile, Bitsy called the police. By the time the cops arrived, the noxious Karen and Kevin were gone.

Martinez showed the officers his video and explained his work assignment. That ended the matter until Martinez's video went viral. Bitsy Brennan soon found herself out of a job as a financial advisor, and junior was charged with assault. The Brennans' stand as instructive examples of why it's prudent to consider all dipsh*ts to be the chronic type unless there are compelling reasons to categorize them as occasional or hybrid.

Dipsh*t analytics for the Brennan bullies:

- **Behavior:** chronic
- **Situation:** benign
- **Cause:** triggered (By – *horrors!* -- a black man in the parking garage.)
- **Outcome:** 4 (damaging) for the Brennans; 3 (disruptive) for Martinez; 2 (imposing) for the police and for Bitsy Brennan's employer, who deemed it prudent to terminate her.

You'll recall that avoid-evade-defend are the recommended tactics for dealing with chronic dipsh*ts. Suppose Martinez had attempted to reason with Bitsy Brennan, as if she were an occasional or hybrid type. If he had said, "You're not a security guard. You shouldn't be interrogating me or demanding my ID," do you think she would have agreed and walked away? If Martinez had said to Edward, "Let's go our separate ways and not have a confrontation," would "slugger" have apologized and backed off? Given that Bitsy reported Martinez to the police for nothing more than his refusal to explain himself, it's unlikely that either she or Edward would have responded favorably to civility and reason.

By assuming that dipsh*ts are the chronic type unless proven otherwise, you instantly clarify the situation and streamline your response. You won't have to ponder the best way to deal with them. You'll know that avoid-evade-defend is your best defense. The Brennans accosted Martinez, so he couldn't avoid them. He could have evaded the confrontation by producing his ID and explaining his work assignment but chose not to. Some might disagree, but I think Martinez acted reasonably when he stood his ground and declined to account for himself. He chose to go immediately into "defend" mode by recording the encounter, and that proved quite effective for him.

Checkout Freakout. At the height of the pandemic, when most businesses enforced a mask mandate, an unknown Karen in Texas went viral when video showed her in a supermarket checkout lane tossing items from her shopping cart in a mask-defiant meltdown. The woman had worn a mask while shopping but removed it as she stood in line. When an employee asked her to put her mask back on, she flew into a rage.

"I don't give a f–k, I'm from Dallas!" she explained. "Dumbass motherf—ing rules and your dumbass motherf—ing s–t…all over a dumbass motherf—ing mask!" Meanwhile, she was holding her mask in her left hand. She stormed out of the store before police could respond.

Meanwhile, a California Karen provided an encore performance in a Trader Joe's. She began shopping without a mask and was informed by store staff that she must mask-up or leave. They ended up escorting her from the store, but not before she unleashed a verbal assault, calling them "Democratic pigs." She told a bystander who was recording the fracas, "I have a breathing problem. My doctor will not let me wear a mask. So anyone harassing me to wear a mask, you guys are violating federal law. Did you get that? Get that on camera."

Dipsh*t analytics for these supermarket scream queens:

- **Behavior:** chronic
- **Situation:** benign (They knew the rules and chose to create drama when reminded to put their masks on.)
- **Cause:** self-induced (Yes, they were triggered when employees asked them to mask-up, but their own non-compliance made intervention by supermarket staff inevitable.)
- **Outcome:** 0 (null) for both Karens, because they suffered negligible consequences; 3 (disruptive) for store personnel who had to confront them, endure their profane abuse, and summon police; 2 (imposing) for other shoppers who were exposed to this.

Sign of the Times. Jaime Toons, a Filipino man, owns a magnificent historic mansion in San Francisco's Pacific Heights neighborhood. One day, as he was stenciling "Black Lives Matter" on the retaining wall in front of his home, a Karen and Kevin couple out for a stroll decided not to mind their own business. Lisa Alexander, CEO of a cosmetic company, approached Toons and asked, "Is this your property? Hi – I'm asking you if this is your property." Alexander's male companion, Robert Larkin, began recording the encounter, as did Toons.

Why are you asking that?' Toons inquired.

"Because this is private property, sir," Larkin replied. "So, are you defacing private property or is this your home? You're free to express your opinions but not on people's property."

Toons refused to explain whether he owned the property, which prompted Alexander to falsely claim that she knew the owners. Fine, Toons retorted – why don't you call the owners? Or call the police if there's any crime to report.

And so, the incident ended as you might expect. Alexander reported Toons to 911. The police arrived only to discover that Toons was the property owner. When the video went viral, Alexander's cosmetic company lost a distributor of its products, and Larkin lost his job with an investment brokerage firm. Alexander later issued a public apology.

Dipsh*t analytics for these self-appointed sign police:

- **Behavior:** chronic
- **Situation:** benign (Toons was stenciling his own wall and bothering no one.)
- **Cause:** triggered (By their unjustified suspiciousness of Toons.)
- **Outcome:** 4 (damaging) for Alexander and Larkin; 2 (imposing) for Toons and for police who had to respond to the scene of this non-crime.

K-9 Karen. One of the most notorious cases of Karen abuse in the United States is the incident between Amy Cooper and Christian Cooper (no relation). Amy Cooper was to become known as the "Central Park Karen."

Their ill-fated encounter began when Christian Cooper asked Amy to leash her unrestrained dog as park regulations required.

She refused, and Christian began recording her as she called 911. "There is an African American man—I am in Central Park—he is recording me and threatening myself and my dog. Please, send the cops immediately!" But Christian's video vindicated him against her accusations.

Both Coopers left the scene before police arrived. The video sparked outrage and widespread notoriety for the Central Park Karen. She lost her job in the aftermath. Meanwhile, Christian Cooper – who was birdwatching when he first encountered Amy Cooper – has been signed by the National Geographic channel to host a birdwatching show.

Dipsh*t analytics for the damsel in faux distress:

- **Behavior:** chronic
- **Situation:** provocative (The dog was off its leash, and she was being challenged about this by a stranger.)
- **Cause:** self-induced (The dog probably didn't remove its own leash.)
- **Outcome:** 5 (destructive) for Amy Cooper, because she lost her job and became a public pariah (she sued her former employer for wrongful termination and lost); 1 (annoying) for Christian Cooper. Because he became famous from this incident and landed a TV contract, he is a rare example of someone who actually benefitted from interacting with a dipsh*t (an exception to the second and ninth laws).

Why Karen and Kevin Create Calamity

Do you recall the case of Hillary Mueller from chapter one? She's the St. Louis woman who blocked a black man from entering her condominium building (and his) until he proved that he lived there by showing his key. Even after she accosted this man unnecessarily and without any authority to do so, she called police and reported that he made her feel "uncomfortable." I guess in her mind "going home while black" is a major provocation.

Karens like Mueller and those profiled in this chapter show themselves to be unpredictable and confrontational. That kind of wildcard toxicity makes it doubly important that we assume each of them to be a chronic type whenever there is any doubt. Few studies on the psychology of Karens and Kevins exist, but there are some theories from psychology and sociology that may explain their rage, entitlement, and free-floating racism.

In view of the Brennans' treatment of Martinez, a brief reconsideration of heuristics and schemas is in order. Their failed intervention demonstrates that reliance on flawed heuristics and schemas can stimulate dipsh*t behavior. Bitsy Brennan's heuristic for "suspected intruder" seems to have been "investigate the intruder." (Of course, she could have been acting on her heuristic for "black man on my turf," but for the moment let's assume neutral intent.)

If the apartment building had a security officer, Brennan's heuristic failed from the get-go. With onsite security, her heuristic should have been, "report intruder to officer on duty." If there was no security, her heuristic could have been "call the police" or even "do nothing." But she and her son acted on an "approach and inquire" heuristic. That might have been reasonable if they had backed off and called the police when Martinez refused to explain himself. Instead, they escalated.

People sometimes report a suspected intruder or prowler who turns out to be a meter reader, a neighbor looking for a lost dog, or some other innocent party. Police would rather investigate false alarms like these than have real threats go unreported. If the Brennans had exited the garage, called the cops, and let the officers determine whether Martinez was legitimately on the premises, there would have been no video, no loss of job for the mother, and no arrest for her son. Bitsy Brennan's "suspected intruder" heuristic was too simplistic for the circumstances and too aggressive. Some might argue that hers was a racist heuristic.

Edward Brennan's heuristic for "uncooperative stranger" was equally unsuitable for the situation. The limitations of "take a swing at him" are self-evident and need no further elaboration. But again, this is why our default position should be to assume each dipsh*t we encounter is the chronic type unless there's overriding evidence to the contrary.

It's likely that both Brennans have adequate schemas for proper behavior during a job interview, when in a theater, or while attending a wedding. But when their "approach and inquire" heuristic failed to extract information from Martinez, the ensuing escalation indicates inadequate schemas for that kind of situation. Rather than aiding them in prudent decision-making, their schemas adversely affected everyone involved.

Obviously, our heuristics and schemas don't always serve us well. Whether or not we prove competent to deal with a particular problem or challenge depends on our knowledge, experience, competence, personality, and the prevailing circumstances. If we are wise, we learn from our failures and do not repeat our mistakes. Instead, we revise and update our heuristics and schemas.

Some sociologists (among then Peggy McIntosh, Patricia Hill Collins, and Michael Kimmel) assert that changing *power dynamics* caused by political, economic, and societal fluctuations can cause privileged groups to feel that their status and power are eroding. When changing times cause advantaged social classes to fear the loss of their preeminence, rage and panic may follow. Their alarmist reactions can foment a backlash against people, policies, or institutions. The Karen and Kevin phenomenon can be explained in part by the destabilizing effects of globalization, economic uncertainty, political strife, shifting demographics, withering away of traditional values, the pandemic, and related macro trends.

Our sense of who we are as individuals is partly determined by our interactions with others, beginning with parents or caregivers, then extended family and friends, and finally people in the wider world. We begin to learn about right and wrong as young children from our immediate family. If we are brought up in a particular religion, chances are we'll remain within that same faith unless we reject religion altogether. As we mature, we learn how to get along with others and make a place for ourselves in society. If we grow up in a violent or racist or xenophobic culture, we will be influenced by the prevailing social norms even if we reject them as repulsive.

Social dominance theory suggests that the behavior of Karens and Kevins reflects the meanings and interpretations they attach to their interactions with people they see as their subordinates – people of color, store employees, or anyone they consider answerable to them. For example, it might be reasonable to suspect that Lisa Alexander and Robert Larkin felt superior to Jaime Toons, the Filipino man stenciling "Black Lives Matter" on his own wall, based on the way they approached him. First, Alexander assumed he couldn't be the owner of the opulent home, then she lectured him about not defacing private property as one might instruct a child, then she lied about knowing who owned the house. Finally, she called the cops when the entire matter was none of her concern. Our attitudes, values, and behaviors do not develop in a vacuum but accrue as a byproduct of our socialization.

You'll notice that Karens and Kevins typically initiate their ill-fated interference with some goal-oriented purpose. The Brennans wanted Martinez to explain his presence in their garage. Hillary Mueller wanted the unnamed black man to prove he lived in the building or else leave. Lisa Alexander and Robert Larkin wanted Toons to stop making his sign on what they assumed was someone else's property. These cases escalated when their targeted victim chose not to submit to their demands.

According to *frustration-aggression theory*, failure to achieve some goal or purpose expresses itself as reactionary hostility. If the source of frustration can't be directly challenged (a boss, for example), then the aggression will remain latent until it is displaced onto a scapegoat. Some Karen or Kevin incidents may be the result of the angry person taking out his or her frustration with life in general on a weak target. But most of these cases appear to be immediate aggression in response to a thwarted demand.

Have you ever seen or heard about someone engaging in racist behavior and then claiming, "I am not a racist!" They may truly believe that. George Zimmerman, the Florida man who shot and killed Trayvon Martin, made that assertion during a Fox News interview. Martin, a black teenager, was walking home from the store one evening, when Zimmerman assumed he was a prowler. Zimmerman, acting as a vigilante, accosted and then shot Martin when he resisted being waylaid by an aggressive stranger.

Symbolic interactionism theory proposes that our attitudes, judgments, and decisions can be influenced by latent biases and stereotypes that lurk beneath our conscious mind. For example, Lisa Alexander and Robert Larkin may have acted on a stereotype about people of color when they challenged Jaime Toons. Apparently, they didn't believe that a Filipino could own a Pacific Heights mansion. And would the Brennans have been concerned about seeing an unknown white man in their parking garage, or was there something about Martinez's appearance that triggered their latent biases?

These are just a few of the theories that can enlighten our understanding of Karens and Kevins. You could also apply these theoretical models to other "villains gone viral," such as combative airline passengers, perpetrators of mass killings, or post-election insurrectionists. As the New Testament advises, "be ye therefore wise as serpents and harmless as doves." Avoid-evade-defend tactics are our best chance of thwarting dipsh*ts whenever they bedevil our lives.

The Florida Man Phenomenon

An even more notorious dipsh*t than Karen or Kevin (if that's even possible) is "Florida Man" – and sometimes "Florida Woman." Headlines abound:

Florida man throws live gator through [restaurant] drive-thru
Florida man insists syringes pulled from his rectum during jail strip search aren't his
Florida man arrested for slapping girlfriend in face with sex toy
Florida man attacks his mother after her dog ate his marijuana
Florida man robs Miami Gardens store with cardboard box on his head
Florida woman arrested for pummeling husband over pickleball dispute
Florida woman rode naked on golf cart through police stand-off with armed suspect
Florida woman drove 19 miles with ex-husband clinging to hood of car
Florida woman accused of battering boyfriend claims his injuries due to "freaky sex"
Florida woman's car caught fire with children inside while she shoplifted in mall

Stay classy, Florida Man and Woman. Your fame precedes you.

The Florida Man/Woman phenomenon is linked to mental health issues in much the same manner than Karens and Kevins are linked to self-centeredness and racism. "Florida out of all the 50 states spends the least amount of money on mental health," according to Andrew King, Ph.D., director the University of North Florida's counseling center. An in-depth investigation by the *Orlando Sentinel* found that an estimated 70% of Floridians lack access to mental health care. *Forbes* ranked the "Worst States for Mental Health," with Florida placing fifth worst. Only Texas, Mississippi, Alabama, and Georgia ranked worse.

Notice, however, that there is no meme for "Texas Man," "Mississippi Man," "Alabama Man," or "Georgia Man" – or any other state for that matter. It's too facile to attribute Florida's reputation for bizarre behavior solely to psychological disorders. Not everyone who misbehaves has a serious mental health condition. And not everyone who has a mental health condition lacks the ability to control his or her conduct. You'll recall from chapter three that most mental disorders do not come with a "free pass" to wreak havoc on the public. Only profoundly impaired individuals – those who are no more competent than children – deserve our forbearance. And even then, we don't have to like it when they create chaos. Everyone else, whatever his or her challenges, owes society decent and law-abiding behavior.

For those Florida Men and Women who do struggle with psychological problems, the *Florida Times-Union* makes a valid point. Reporter Ben Conark observes:

> The criminal justice system and mental health are intertwined and inseparable. So many of the people arrested on any given day in Florida are dealing with mental illness or extreme poverty. So I think when you look at it through that lens, it's pretty obvious that a lot of what seems zany or weird on the surface is actually pretty sad when you come to grips with the circumstances of what these people are really dealing with.

There is a paradox in balancing Conark's empathy with the recognition that victims of dipsh*ttery deserve our compassion too. Do we excuse toxic perpetrators who may be struggling with mental health issues, poverty, unemployment, or any number of social ills? Or do we side with the victims and thereby risk demonizing people who may not be "bad" but merely "damaged"?

I think the sensible approach requires seeking a balance. That's why I believe most people, regardless of their personal challenges and struggles, should be expected to conform to decent and lawful behavior. Otherwise, we risk enabling the use of mental health as an excuse for those who don't want to limit their behavior to acceptable standards. On the other hand, I advocate leniency and compassion for people who are not mentally competent, even when their misbehavior causes problems. We don't have to approve of their destructiveness, but we can insist that the police, justice system, and social services programs deal with them fairly.

Here's a Florida Man who I believe has earned his dipsh*t label fair and square. According to Clearwater police, Taylor William Beverly, age 22, ran a stop light on his motorcycle, then fled when officers tried to pull him over. During the chase, Beverly ran several more stop lights and reached speeds topping 100 miles per hour. Beverly was not alone on his motorcycle. Seated behind him, his female companion was holding on for dear life and screaming for him to stop. They were on their first date.

Police soon called off the chase rather than risk fatalities. But they cornered Beverly later at an intersection. When asked to explain himself, the scofflaw said he was just trying to "show off" for his date. No doubt he made quite an impression.

Beverly's conduct doesn't strike me as mental health related. It seems more like pure, unadulterated dipsh*ttery, possibly fueled by immaturity, recklessness, impulsiveness, testosterone, and low conscientiousness. I wouldn't be surprised if intoxicating substances were a factor. But this is all speculation. We can recognize stupid and irresponsible behavior without having to fully understand it. Even so, the following theories may explain the senselessness of Florida Man/Woman's legendary malfeasance.

We all act impulsively at times, but some people are temperamentally predisposed to yield to their urges without considering alternatives or weighing consequences. For them, *impulsivity theory* maintains that spontaneous acting-without-thinking is an aspect of their personalities. We don't know whether Beverly is an impulsivity-prone individual or if his decision to take his date on a high-speed police chase was an isolated incident. This is why the fourth law recommends assuming all dipsh*ts are chronic types unless you know better. Assume the worst and protect yourself.

Many of those who engage in dangerous driving, substance abuse, compulsive gambling, reckless spending, and unprotected sex are impulsivity-prone individuals. One of the diagnostic criteria for borderline personality disorder is a pattern of impulsive and self-destructive behavior. Not all impulsivity-prone people are borderlines, but borderlines are at high risk for reckless conduct. And impulsivity is a breeding ground for dipsh*ttery.

Just as some people are naturally impulsive, *risk-taking theory* maintains that others are predisposed to recklessness. They have an above average tolerance for taking chances, and they enjoy the thrill of dangerous behavior. Without that stimulation they can become bored and restless. When channeled intelligently, risk-taking can be productive, as entrepreneurs and investors know. Too often, however, it devolves into tragedy.

Consider the case of Benjamin Nathaniel Bruce, age 23, of Perth, Australia. He's charged with an astounding 64 counts of sexual abuse against nine women he met via online dating apps. During the investigation, A police commissioner said that officers "found a significant amount of images and videos on devices, and the special crime team is currently working through those images to see if we can identify more [victims]."

If the charges against him are true, Bruce epitomizes someone abnormally tolerant of risk and undeterred by consequences. Frequent high-risk behavior is one of the criteria for antisocial personality disorder and would apply to borderlines as well. Reckless risk-takers tend to engage in the same kind of perilous behaviors as those who are impulsivity-prone. Some types of risk involve planning and forethought, but impulsivity by definition lacks premeditation.

Manifestations of the Fourth Law

This chapter began with Amsterdam's enjoinder against young British men. It is therefore fitting to conclude with the indiscretions of dipsh*ts abroad. If boorish behavior while traveling were an Olympic sport, Americans would take home a medal every time.

Each year, Yellowstone National Park makes a point of warning visitors not to approach bears, bison or elk. A baby bison had to be euthanized after a tourist's manhandling of the animal caused it to be rejected by the herd. More often, these ignoramuses find themselves on the business end of an angry bull or she-bear. Elsewhere, officials in Cabo San Lucas have begun warning

108

tourists not to emulate "influencers" by swimming with killer whales. And recently a video posted to social media showed a man on safari in the Serengeti reaching out of a vehicle to pet a passing lioness. Incidents such as these demarcate the point at which dipsh*ttery crosses over into Darwin Awards territory.

I lived in New Orleans for many years. Even during the 1990s, when the Crescent City's murder rate regularly ranked as number one or two among U.S. cities, I enjoyed living there, although I took precautions. I usually didn't go out at night except in well-lit, highly trafficked areas, such as the French Quarter. Countless times I've known of tourists doing foolish things like wandering drunk down a dark side street and meeting with disaster. But I no longer live there, nor would I want to.

Since the pandemic, crime has raged out of control. Carjackings are rampant, as are smash-and-grab robberies of parked vehicles. Murder is back to 1990s levels, and the city's leadership seems feckless and adrift. Random, drive-by shooting on I-10 are now a threat, so even traversing the city without stopping is risky. Meanwhile, the municipal government can't even fill potholes or send out accurate water bills. Shootings in the French Quarter, which were a rarity when I lived there, are now a recurring event.

A visitor form Denmark, for example, might not be aware of the Big Easy's plunge into criminal near-anarchy. It's one thing to visit a city without realizing the severity of local crime, but it's quite another to behave in a way that invites victimization. But one Dane did just that.

The Danish tourist arrived in town with a group of friends. Now, see how many red flags you can spot: One evening, he separated from his companions and picked up a prostitute in the French Quarter. He didn't have a car to drive her to a hotel, so he got into her car. She drove him to a part of town no tourist or safety-conscious local should visit, especially at night. The next morning his body was found in the weeds beside a litter-strewn back street. He had been shot in the head. All his valuables were missing. The moral of this story is that failing to heed obvious risks can ruin your whole day. And don't be a dipsh*t, especially in a strange town.

New Orleans is just one of many U.S. cities that has endured a crime surge in recent years. Still, it's a city that I know well and which is a top U.S. tourist and convention destination. It and other crime-plagued metropolises have seen citizens' quality of life demolished by a criminal element that we must regard as chronic types pursuant to the fourth law.

As for young British men, if you're willing to risk your life but Amsterdam doesn't want you, New Orleans still beckons. You can stumble around drunk in the French Quarter, and no one will complain if you p*ss or puke in the Mississippi. Just remember to stand perfectly still whenever a mass shooting starts. That way your demise will be quick and painless.

* * *

"Think of how stupid the average person is, and realize half of them are stupider than that."
– George Carlin

Chapter Six

The Fifth Law: A Dipsh*t is as Likely as Anyone Else to Become his or her Own Victim

Kayla Norton, 25, and Jose Torres, 26, were part of a group that adorned their pickup trucks with Confederate flags and paraded around the suburbs of Atlanta to "celebrate the flag's heritage." No sooner had the truck posse hit the streets than black motorists began reporting threats and racial slurs from the group. Eventually these neo-Confederates happened upon an outdoor birthday party for an 8-year-old African-American child.

The rampaging rednecks screamed racial slurs at the birthday celebrants and brandished weapons, even as someone pleaded, "This is a child's birthday party!" Police responded but initially made no arrests. Later, the lot of them were charged with making terroristic threats. (Georgia doesn't have a hate crimes statute.)

Norton and Torres' racist bravado was noticeably muted when a jury found them both guilty. They wept as the judge sentenced them to a combined 19 years in prison under Georgia's street gang terrorism law. Other members of the group (15 in all) were previously convicted and sentenced.

What a farrago of fiendishness. This criminal mischief was needless, malicious, and stupid. And while many blacks were frightened by the armed threats, the greatest victims of the debacle were the racists themselves.

Dipsh*t analytics for these rebels without a clue:

- **Behavior:** chronic
- **Situation:** benign (There was no trouble until they stirred it up.)
- **Cause:** habitual (Because of course they are.)
- **Outcome:** 5 (destructive) for the mouth-breathing knuckle-draggers; 3 (disruptive) for those threatened; 2 (imposing) for the police, prosecutor, and court.

The mentality of these Georgia misfits (my people, sad to say) is mirrored in a sizeable portion of the "Make American Great Again" (MAGA) cult. I use the word "cult," because January 6 2021 proved that many within that movement are willing to do anything -- even bring down the government – at Trump's behest. As of this writing, over one thousand J6 insurrectionists have been charged, and about half that number have been sentenced. Like the Atlanta pickup posse, those who assaulted the Capitol ended up as victims of their own dipsh*ttery.

Compare the J6 jihadists to the Georgia group:

- **Behavior:** chronic
- **Situation:** provocative
- **Cause:** triggered (But many were probably habitual.)
- **Outcome:** 5 (destructive) for those charged and convicted and for the one protester who was killed (likewise for their families); 4 or 5 (damaging or destructive) for police who were attacked, depending on how they were affected long-

term; 4 (damaging) for lawmakers and staff who had to flee for their lives and hide; 3 (disruptive) for the personnel who had to clean up and repair damage to the Capitol, for the justice system that had to track down and prosecute hundreds of insurrectionists, and for all law-abiding citizens who witnessed a near coup d'état.

Norton, Torres, and their fellow Confederate flag-wavers told themselves that they were setting out to celebrate the "heritage" of Southern rebellion. The truck parade was a travesty that quickly descended into criminal mischief and intimidation. The "celebrating heritage" pretense allowed them to rationalize their behavior as historic or patriotic.

In 1979 psychologists Henri Tajfel and John Turner introduced *social identity theory* which explains how we develop a sense of identity within social groups and how group influence affects our behavior toward others. Besides our individual identities, we also have social identities based on the groups we identify with (e.g., nationality, gender, ethnicity, religion, occupation, political party, and so on). Someone who is attracted to white supremacist ideas and beliefs will naturally gravitate to friends and cliques who support and reinforce that racist mindset.

Social identity theory proposes that Norton and Torres' individual and social identities would become bonded to their in-group of like-minded bigots. Acceptance within that group would depend on matching the racism and viciously outspoken behavior of the other members. And even if Norton and Torres had no intention of harassing blacks when they joined the truck parade, they would have felt considerable peer pressure to mimic the others rather than remain silent. That's why Norton, for example, could threaten blacks and yet tell their families at her sentencing, "I want you all to know that that is not me. That is not me." She may very well be a passive racist who allowed herself to be pressured into overt aggression on this occasion by her peers.

Another aspect of social identity theory that applies to this case is the tendency of many people to favor those who are "like them" – that is, people they regard as belonging to the same in-group. Anyone outside the group is held in lower esteem or even despised. Extremists of all stripes often take their devaluation of out-groups too far. When dislike descends into demonization, as it did with the Georgia white supremacists, group members can become dangerous.

We should be grateful that mainstream society now repudiates racist ideas and behavior. However, this rejection can lead people like Norton and Torres to feel persecuted for their beliefs. They may come to see themselves as victims, even though it's their own noxious conduct that has made them outcasts. According to social identity theory, people who feel persecuted (whether rightly or wrongly) are prone to committing reactionary violence.

Individuals with high *social dominance orientation* (SDO) support and advocate inequality among social classes. They tolerate privileges for some groups and discrimination against others. SDO can be measured on a scale from low to high, with high scorers supporting a rigid social hierarchy. Most white supremacists, for example, would earn high SDO scores in keeping with their preference for white dominance and black subjugation.

Psychologists Jim Sidanius and Felicia Pratto introduced the SDO concept as part of their *social dominance theory*. While social identity theory addresses interactions between people and groups, social domination theory explores how groups relate to each other in their struggle for relevance and power in society. Some groups, as we know, enjoy more status and have more clout than others. Laws, social norms, and institutions facilitate hierarchies and legitimize the existing social order. But eventually change does come, regardless of entrenched power and privilege. Previously marginalized groups such as minorities and the LGTBQ community have gained more power, while people like Norton and Torres are seeing their cherished white supremacy slipping away.

Begin Self-Destruct Sequence

Norton, Torres, and their cohort of racists vividly demonstrate the principle that people who commit obtuse, offensive acts frequently become their own victims. But there are many other contenders clamoring to serve as poster children for the principle that dipsh*ts are likely to self-victimize. Consider, for example, disruptive airline passengers, who have become a plague for flight crews and well-behaved travelers. The Federal Aviation Administration (FAA) received reports of 1,009 unruly passenger incidents in 2020, an astounding 5,973 incidents (a 492% increase) in 2021, and 2,455 in 2022. Mask protests at the height of the pandemic probably account for much of 2021's spike.

Late for the sky: Vicki Meyers, age 53, didn't want to miss her flight from Phoenix Sky Harbor Airport to St. Louis. Unfortunately, the doors to the jetway had closed by the time she reached the gate. Not one to give up at the first obstacle, Meyers reportedly sprinted through employees-only doors and made a dash for the runway. She hurried past signs that read, "no trespassing" and "felony" in English and Spanish, making a beeline for her departing aircraft. Ground crew personnel rushed to intercept and detain her until police could be summoned.

Meyers allegedly admitted to the arresting officer that she wanted to stop the plane and board it. She is charged with criminal trespassing and remains free pending trial. In his song, "Late for the Sky," Jackson Browne posed the musical question, "How long have I been running for that morning flight through the whispered promises and the changing light?" Perhaps Meyers knows the answer.

Dipsh*t analytics for Vicki "Feets Don't Fail Me Now" Meyers:

- **Behavior:** chronic
- **Situation:** frenetic (Anyone who's arrived at the gate after the doors have closed will understand.)
- **Cause:** triggered
- **Outcome:** 4 (damaging) for Meyers who now faces criminal charges; 3 (disruptive) for ground crew staff who had to intercept and detain her; 2 (imposing) for the police, prosecutor, and court.

Red in tooth and claw. Here's a brain teaser for you – take all the time you need: Which is easier and better for you in the long run, to get off a plane when asked by the flight crew and police, or to be dragged bodily off the plane, thrown in jail, and prosecuted? Simone Bryna Kim, age 24, chose the latter answer and punctuated her response with biting and scratching.

Kim boarded a flight from Miami to Philadelphia, and promptly got into an argument with a fellow passenger. "I will f*** you up!" Kim allegedly threatened. When the flight crew attempted to eject her, she refused to disembark. Police then attempted to gain her cooperation, but there was some part of "get off or go to jail" that apparently didn't register with her. And so officers dragged her away, kicking and screaming.

People magazine reported that, "Kim currently faces two felony charges of battery on a police officer, one felony charge of resisting an officer with violence, three misdemeanor counts of assault on a police officer and a misdemeanor trespassing charge." On the plus side, her Florida vacation was extended at no cost courtesy of the Miami-Dade Police Department.

Dipsh*t analytics for combative Kim:

- **Behavior:** chronic
- **Situation:** benign (Nothing was amiss until she boarded the plane and started arguing.)
- **Cause:** habitual (When she says, "I will f*** you up," I believe her.)
- **Outcome:** 4 or 5 (damaging or destructive) for Kim, whose score will depend on the severity of her punishment, given that she's facing multiple felonies; 3 (disruptive) for passengers and crew; 3 (damaging) for the police officers that she injured; 2 (imposing) for the prosecutor and court.

Jail Brittania. Aboard a charter flight from Cancun, Mexico back to the U.K., Anthony Joseph James Kirby and Damien Jake Murphy caused such a disturbance that the pilot decided to divert to Maine and offload them. They spewed racial slurs, assaulted a flight attendant, and slapped another passenger. The pilot didn't want to start the long flight across the Atlantic with these raging troublemakers on board.

Flight attendants noticed that the men seemed to be "slightly intoxicated" when they boarded, so they were denied alcohol during the flight. This apparently set them off. They removed a bottle of gin from a carry-on bag and began drinking from it. When the cabin crew demanded that they surrender the bottle, the men became more aggressive. The captain repeatedly warned them to no avail before diverting the flight.

Police met the plane at Bangor International Airport and arrested the hooligans. After spending a little over two months in jail, they were convicted and sentenced to time served. The court ordered them to pay $26,589 in fines and costs. Next year, Amsterdam!

Dipsh*t analytics for the boozing Brits:

- **Behavior:** chronic
- **Situation:** benign
- **Cause:** self-induced (They could be habitual, but I'll cut them a scintilla of slack.)
- **Outcome:** 4 (damaging) for the noxious drunks, who had to spend a few weeks in a foreign jail and must pay substantial fines; (3) disruptive for the airline, the flight crew,

and the other passengers; (2) imposing for Bangor's police, prosecutor, and court.

Mr. Smooth. The lady seated next to him aboard their Alaska Airlines flight thought Adam David Seymour, age 37, seemed friendly. As the plane climbed to cruising altitude, he removed three small bottles from his carry-on and began drinking. He then ordered two rounds of Jack Daniels. Before long, the noticeably intoxicated Seymour began touching and groping her. She told investigators that he said she "looked like a lesbian" and "we're all going to die." Then he lit up a cigarette.

The woman managed to slip a message to people in the seats in front of her – who just happened to be off-duty cops. The officers alerted the flight crew, and they moved the frightened passenger to another seat. Seymour then reportedly began shoving and threatening a male passenger, telling him, "I'm going to kill you." The cops put Seymour in flex cuffs and moved him to a jump seat away from passengers.

Upon arrival in Anchorage, Seymour was arrested by airport police. They swabbed his hands which tested positive for cocaine residue. He was charged with assault with intent to commit a felony.

Dipsh*t analytics for "See More" Jail Time:

- **Behavior:** chronic
- **Situation:** benign
- **Cause:** self-induced
- **Outcome:** 4 or 5 (damaging or destructive) for Seymour, depending on the severity of his punishment; 3 (disruptive) for his female victim as well as the passengers and

flight crew who had to deal with his dipsh*ttery; 2 (imposing) for the police, prosecutor, and court.

Knockin' on Heaven's Door. It's good to have standards. Tiffany Michelle Miles, age 36, of Washington, D.C. certainly has hers, and settling for slow beverage service isn't one of them. Seated in first class, Miles reportedly became incensed that the libations weren't flowing freely enough. In an apparent attempt to take her complaint directly to the captain, Miles made a dash for the cockpit door.

Kara Rosario, a fellow passenger, told reporters that ""she was yelling that she paid for first class and that she's not getting her drink that she's ordered." Meanwhile, the captain alerted Air Traffic Control that the "subject is currently on the loose in the cabin." The flight was diverted to Raleigh-Durham International Airport, where police were waiting to arrest her. Miles caught a huge break when the local district attorney, for reasons unknown, dropped the charges.

Dipsh*t analytics for Tiffany Michelle "Cocktail or Cockpit" Miles:

- **Behavior:** chronic
- **Situation:** benign
- **Cause:** self-induced
- **Outcome:** 4 (damaging) for Miles, who escaped prosecution but was arrested and thrown in jail – where beverage service is notoriously slow; 3 (disruptive) for the airline, flight crew, and passengers; 2 (imposing) for the police, prosecutor, and court.

Tore His Mind on a Jagged Sky. Francisco Severo Torres, age 33, created a bit of a stir aboard a United flight from Los Angeles to Boston. He tried to open the cabin door mid-flight. This was not well-received by fellow passengers and the crew.

It seems obvious from video and eyewitness accounts that Torres suffered a psychotic break. In fact, his bizarre behavior continued after his arrest and even during court appearances. The judge ordered a mental health evaluation.

See for yourself. These are some examples of the "word salad" Torres uttered during the flight:

> Where are they diverting us? Because wherever they do, there's going to be a bloodbath everywhere. You can run away if you want. I won't kill you...I'm Balthazar. Or put up your hands, because I'm Balthazar...since I'm taking over this plane.

Torres reportedly attacked two flight attendants, stabbing one in the neck with a spoon. Passengers had to restrain him until the flight landed.

The dipsh*t label does not apply in the Torres case. He appears to have been profoundly mentally disturbed and cognitively incompetent during this episode. If I had been aboard that plane, I would have been just as afraid and angry as the other passengers. But as ethical, humane individuals, we should not apply insulting labels to people for debilitating conditions which they did not choose. But that doesn't mean we have to condone or minimize the disastrous outcome of someone's horrific conduct.

The common threads running through the white supremacist and disruptive passenger cases are their craven selfishness, lack of empathy for others, and remarkably immature behavior. Such childish, emotional reasoning and moral ignorance are at the level we would expect of a small child. That's a stunning insight into the mental landscape of these supposedly competent adults.

Cognitive-behavioral theory (CBT) holds that deficient cognitive powers, such as reliance on primitive, emotional reasoning, makes one susceptible to overestimating his or her competence or underestimating potential negative consequences. CBT emphasizes that distorted thinking and impaired judgment may lead people to act recklessly or outrageously. This theory aligns quite well with dipsh*t analytics, because both attempt to explain how people's thoughts, beliefs, and interpretations of situations influence their behavior.

Another common characteristic of the racists and disruptive passengers described in this chapter is impulsivity (which you read about in chapter five). When someone tends to act on immediate urges or desires without considering potential consequences, that person is likely to plunge headlong into disasters. Most of us have enough self-inhibiting skills to govern our reckless passions and curtail gross irresponsibility. But this self-restraint ability is impaired in impulsivity-prone individuals. How many times have we heard that someone "just snapped" and committed a violent crime? In some cases, the backstory may be that the person is naturally predisposed toward impulsive behavior, and something just happened to trigger them.

The first law of dipsh*ttery, as you'll recall, states that every person has an inner dipsh*t trying to get out and run amok. Each chapter of this book presents true cases paired with psychological and sociological theories that explain stupid and despicable behavior. But in the end, dumb, disruptive people are a fact of life. Most of us cross over into that territory at one time or another ourselves. Like death and taxes, it's inevitable.

Three Brains and Still Dumb as a Bag of Hammers

Knowing something about personality disorders and their associated symptoms and behaviors (see chapter three) can help us recognize behavioral cues and understand the challenges of people with those conditions. Of course, we must recognize that not everyone who behaves outrageously has a personality disorder. And snap judgments about someone's mental health often miss the mark, especially when we jump to conclusions as "armchair psychologists." But I maintain that it's better to know something about personality disorders than to remain perpetually perplexed by aberrant behavior.

While we all have different mental landscapes, every intact human brain has the same tri-level structure. Paul D. Maclain, M.D. in the 1960s introduced the concept of the "triune brain" consisting of a primitive reptilian brain, a more developed paleomammalian brain, and an advanced neomammalian brain. Each of these structures has a role to play in causing dipsh*t behavior or allowing it to happen.

The reptilian brain controls our animalistic drives, such as sexual desire and territoriality, as well as our survival needs, such as balance, hunger and thirst, and regulation of breathing and heartbeat. Consisting of the basal ganglia and brain stem, this part of our brains can trigger aggression, recklessness, and even violence. Consider, for example, the "Karens" who approached unfamiliar black men without cause and demanded that they account for themselves. Such behavior illustrates reptilian territoriality in action: *What's someone like you doing on my turf?* But that's when our more advanced cranial faculties should kick in.

Next in evolutionary development is the paleomammalian brain, which physician and neuroscientist, Andrew E. Budson, describes as regulating "our motivation, emotions, and memory, including behavior such as parenting." The hypothalamus, hippocampus, amygdala, and cingulate cortex make up this ancient mammalian structure. When we encounter reckless, incompetent, or offensive behavior, paleomammalian emotion and motivation combined with unthinking reptilian aggression may be the dual-action cause. Tanner Cook, the YouTuber who was shot by Alan Colie while Cook harassed the man for a social media video, is an example of someone manifesting the willfulness and motivation of the paleomammalian brain combined with reptilian cruelty and aggression.

Thank goodness we have a more-developed brain structure that can control these inferior structures -- "one brain to rule them all," as J.R.R. Tolkien might have said if he had been a neuroscientist. Our neomammalian brain (the neocortex) enables reasoning, judgment, conceptual thought, language, and self-restraint based on moral, ethical, or legal constraints. When people speak of using "critical thinking" or "higher-order reasoning skills," they are invoking the neomammalian brain's superpowers. If a man skilled in martial arts walks away from a drunk who takes a swing at him in a bar (rather than turning the aggressor's body into a bloody pulp), he is using his advanced brain structure to override the primitive drives and emotions of his reptilian and paleomammalian brains.

Bear in mind, the concept of a triune brain is rudimentary. For example, it does not take into account the role of hormones and the sympathetic and parasympathetic nervous systems in stimulating and regulating human behavior. Nor does it describe the functions of the brain's hemispheres or the corpus callosum, which carries signals between them. But it's helpful to know, for example, that aggression, territoriality, and sexual jealously are products of the reptilian brain, even if one does not know that epinephrine and norepinephrine may also act as stimulants.

The criminal racists and out-of-control airline passengers profiled in this chapter exemplify our primitive brain functions when not regulated by what Lincoln called "the better angels of our natures." But one need not be a white supremacist or crazed flyer to become victims of one's own dipsh*ttery. Below are a few cases – all different – that also exemplify this principle.

At least he shot the bad guy. Justin McCall, a classic "Florida man," burglarized several homes and vehicles while out on bond for previous burglaries. He was also on parole for theft of a firearm. In one of the vehicles, McCall, age 28, found a handgun, which he stole.

McCall held the purloined pistol in his hand while rummaging through another vehicle. Somehow he managed to discharge the weapon and shoot himself in the leg. McCall went to a nearby home for help, and police rushed to the scene. While McCall was receiving treatment for his wound, the cops viewed security videos provided by several homeowners. That's all the evidence they needed to charge him with 13 crimes.

Karma finally caught up with McCall at sentencing. Florida law mandates tough punishment for crimes committed with a firearm. By shooting himself with the stolen gun, McCall triggered (no pun intended) the harsher sentencing guidelines. He drew a 20-year prison term, and if that's not dipsh*t justice, I'll kiss your cheeks (the big ones).

Dipsh*t analytics for Deadeye McCall:

- **Behavior:** chronic
- **Situation:** benign
- **Cause:** self-induced
- **Outcome:** 5 (destructive) for McCall; 4 (damaging) for the people who had their cars broken into and homes burglarized; 2 (imposing) for medical providers, police, prosecutor, and court.

Man of Letters. Randy Frasinelli, age 66, faced charges of fraudulently obtaining $3.8 million in Paycheck Protection Program (PPP) loans during the pandemic. Undeterred by his arrest, Frasinelli applied for an additional half million dollars in PPP loans while out on bond. He spent the money on an African safari, expensive art, and several luxury vehicles, to name but a few of his extravagances. Frasinelli ultimately pleaded guilty to bank fraud and money laundering. But that's not where his chicanery ended. From the *Pittsburg Tribune-Review*:

> As far as character letters go, Randy Frasinelli submitted the best. They came from corporate executives, nonprofit groups and an

Ivy League university. There's one from the bishop of the Diocese of Pittsburgh. And another from Leadership Pittsburgh.

There's even one from former Allegheny County Executive Jim Roddey. Well, it was supposed to be from him. But, if it was, Roddey spelled his own name wrong – twice. According to the federal government, all of the letters are fake.

In preparation for his sentencing hearing, Frasinelli allegedly forged 13 character reference letters to the judge. Prosecutors are now urging a harsher sentence in view of the con man's attempt to defraud the court. Said Frasinelli's defense counsel in a memorandum to the judge: "He has always done things in a very big way."

Dipsh*t analytics for Forge-i-nelli:

- **Behavior:** chronic
- **Situation:** provocative (He was about to be sentenced and desperate for any relief.)
- **Cause:** habitual (His fraudulent behavior seems to be relentless.)
- **Outcome:** 5 (destructive) for Frasinelli since he only made his predicament worse; 2 (imposing) for the police, prosecutor, his defense attorney, and the court; 3 (disruptive) for people who had to disavow that letters written in their name were forged.

Keep watching the skies. Someone needs to break the news to David Dodd of Sheffield, England that aliens communicate via telepathy, not laser pens. Dodd, age 60, received a six-month suspended sentence for shining his laser pen at a police helicopter.

He testified that he thought the chopper was a UFO and that he was trying to communicate with the aliens.

According to the prosecutor, Dodd subjected the pilot to a 40-minute assault with his laser pen, and officers aboard the helicopter had to resort to protective eye gear. In his defense, Dodd's attorney was reduced to arguing that his client "had a reasonable belief it was something extraterrestrial" and that "dazzling the occupants of that helicopter" was the furthest thing from his mind. I'm sure the helicopter crew was less than dazzled with Dodd's visual assault.

Dipsh*t analytics for Dodgy Dodd:

- **Behavior:** chronic
- **Situation:** benign (No evidence that the "aliens" sought contact from Dodd.)
- **Cause:** self-induced
- **Outcome:** 3 (disruptive) for Dodd and also for the helicopter crew; 2 (imposing) for the police, prosecutor, and court.

My Experience with a Self-Defeating Dipsh*t

Here's a case from my own experience regarding an instructor who proved to be her own worst enemy. Before my retirement, when I was a university dean, one of my occupational hazards was listening to students gripe about their professors. One day, my administrative assistant walked into my office with a startled look on her face. She explained that a group of about 15 students was in the outer office demanding to see me about their sociology instructor. That amounted to about half the class.

Students showing up en masse to complain is both a rare and extreme occurrence. I stepped into the outer office and greeted the mob of angry complainants. I told them that I would meet with three of them and asked that they take a few minutes to choose their spokespersons. The rest of them could wait in the hallway.

A few minutes later their three delegates came forward, and once we were all comfortably seated, they told me the following story. With the semester in session for only five weeks, their instructor had already skipped two classes. Not only didn't she show up, but she didn't notify anyone either. She was required to report any absences or class cancellations to me, and my administrative assistant would then notify the students. Most faculty members don't miss two classes in an entire semester.

The instructor's absences counted as the "good news," because the accusations were about to get worse. After the first few sessions, the instructor began dismissing each class 10 to 15 minutes early. She also had made insulting remarks to one of the students, which led to a shouting match. Another professor who was trying to teach in an adjacent classroom intervened and asked the instructor to keep the noise down – and she got into a shouting match with him in the hallway.

If even half of the students' claims were true, this situation demanded drastic action. I went out and asked the students who were waiting if they agreed with what I'd been told. They all swore that the allegations were true. I told them that I would handle the matter and gave them my word that these problems would not be allowed to continue. But I needed one more thing from them – a written and signed statement of grievances. I told them to return in 24 hours, and I'd have a document ready for their signatures. I emphasized that I would need at least ten of them to sign if these accusations were to carry any weight. The next day they all returned and signed.

I then spoke with the professor whom she had argued with in the hallway. He agreed that she seemed out-of-control on that one occasion. He also said he'd noticed that she was dismissing her classes early. His class started at the same time, and her classroom was usually dark and empty by the time his class ended. Now I was certain that the students' accusations were true and that any disciplinary action I might take would stand up if she appealed.

Next, I met with another of our professors who was qualified to teach that sociology class. I explained the crisis at hand and the urgent need to terminate her. He already had a full schedule, but I wanted to know if he'd be willing to take over the sociology class as a replacement for our off-the-rails instructor. He readily agreed. Now I was prepared to go *mano a mano* with the dipsh*t instructor.

The woman in question was an adjunct faculty member. An adjunct is a part-timer hired to teach for one semester only. Most universities employ adjuncts on an as-needed, semester-by-semester basis. They're basically "temps." This instructor was newly hired and teaching her first class for us.

I called her in for a meeting and showed her the written statement of grievances signed by her students. She started making excuses, and I cut her off. "This isn't going to work – even if they are wrong. With half your students in rebellion, there's no way you can effectively teach that class. And I've already confirmed that you've missed classes without telling me and dismissed classes early. Those reasons alone require that I remove you."

Her own irresponsible, incompetent, and irrational behavior led to the loss of her teaching assignment and precluded her from being considered for future employment at the university. Many of our adjuncts received continuing offers to teach semester after semester, and they usually received hiring preference when a full-time faculty position opened up. So she sacrificed a lot by abusing the trust of the university, her students, and me. Her behavior was especially puzzling, because she had taught successfully at other colleges and came highly recommended.

Dipsh*t analytics for this feckless faculty failure:

- **Behavior:** hybrid (Her prior employment history was clean, so this was an isolated situation.)
- **Situation:** benign
- **Cause:** self-induced
- **Outcome:** 4 (damaging) for the instructor; 3 (disruptive) for the students in that class and for me in having to fire her and then replace her mid-semester; 2 (imposing) for the professor she shouted at and whose class she disrupted, and also for the professor who had to take over her class on short notice.

Recognizing stupid, despicable behavior when it occurs and applying dipsh*t analytics in real time will allow you to assess situational risk and, if possible, avoid becoming collateral damage. To develop a habit of using these analytics, it's helpful to analyze cases in hindsight, as I am doing throughout this book. But you'll need to analyze in real time if you are to make avoid-evade-defend decisions at the critical moment.

* * *

"Sometimes a man wants to be stupid, if it lets him do a thing his cleverness forbids."
– John Steinbeck

Chapter Seven

The Sixth Law: Whom the Gods wish to Destroy They First Make a Dipsh*t

You may know the maxim, "whom the gods wish to destroy they first make mad." The source of this bit of wisdom is murky. It has been attributed to Sophocles, Aeschylus, and Euripides. Two 17th century intellectuals, Jacques Duport and Joshua Barnes, both claimed authorship. Jean-Jacques Rousseau quoted a Latin version of the adage in 1769, and it appeared in an 1854 book by William Anderson Scott, a clergyman. The phrase also appears in Henry Wadsworth Longfellow's poem, *The Masque of Pandora* (1875). It's an idea of long endurance despite its dubious ancestry.

You need not trouble yourself about the origin of, "whom the gods wish to destroy they first make a dipsh*t." I am the father of that *bon mot*. I admit to having borrowed (i.e., stolen) the essence of the sixth law from ancient sages. In my defense, I hasten to point out that I only pilfer from the best.

The gods certainly made a dipsh*t of Reverend Ted Haggard, though he'd probably blame Satan. In the early 2000s Haggard was at the summit of his power. Pastor of a megachurch in Colorado Springs, Colorado, and president of the National Association of Evangelicals, Haggard was a frequent guest at the George W. Bush White House. His charisma and dynamic preaching made him popular among the faithful. However, in a stunning turn of events, Haggard's ministry self-destructed when an accuser came forward, claiming that Haggard engaged in a gay sexual affair and used methamphetamine. He resigned in disgrace and left the state.

The scandal unfolded in November 2006, when Mike Jones, a male escort, claimed that he had assignations with Haggard for three years. These allegations were doubly damning, because Haggard's evangelical faith taught that gay sex is a sin. Haggard himself preached against it.

Additional revelations – and not the biblical kind – soon came to light. CNN reported that Haggard "sought drugs from a young male volunteer at his Colorado church and masturbated in front of him in a hotel room." Grant Haas, the volunteer, said, "[Haggard] really thought he was invincible, because he used to say to me, 'You know what, Grant, you can become a man of God and you can have a little bit of fun on the side.'" Haas received a six-figure settlement from New Life Church.

Years later, Haggard founded St. James Church and attempted to put the past behind him. But in 2012 a church member struggling with heroin addiction accused Haggard of asking him to procure methamphetamine. According to MinistryWatch, a church elder confronted Haggard about this allegation, whereupon "Haggard acknowledged the purchase and reportedly handed over a briefcase containing methamphetamine, a 'well-used' pipe, a sex toy, and gay porn.'"

For whatever reason, Haggard was allowed to remain as minister at St. James, because new allegations from that congregation arose against him in 2019. Haggard engaged in "questionable touching with young males, according to videotaped claims from two St. James members," MinistryWatch reported. Haggard denied the allegations but left St. James and now conducts religious services in his home. He reportedly has plans to offer a youth ministry in his basement, where kids can hang out, play games, and shoot pool. What could possibly go wrong?

Dish*t analytics for Two-Faced Ted:

- **Behavior:** chronic (Haggard is a near-miss for the hybrid label, because of his track record of accomplishment. But his extreme recklessness with extramarital sex and drugs affects more than one area of his life. Also, the recent allegations indicate that he may not have learned his lesson.)
- **Situation:** benign
- **Cause:** habitual (I'm giving credence to his alleged malfeasance at St. James.)
- **Outcome:** 5 (destructive for Haggard and his family; 4 (damaging) for the people he exploited in his role as their pastor; 3 (disruptive) for church elders who had to clean up the aftermath of Haggard's shenanigans; 3 or 4 (disruptive of damaging) for members of Haggard's various congregations, depending on the spiritual, psychological, and financial impact of Haggard's deception.

Not since the fall of Jim and Tammy Faye Bakker in the 1980s has such a prominent and powerful evangelical minister fallen from celestial heights to such depraved depths. The Bakkers founded the nationally televised PTL Club ("Praise the Lord") show and served as its hosts. They used this platform to raise money for developing and expanding Heritage USA, a Christian-themed ersatz Disneyland.

Behind the scenes, meanwhile, chicanery was afoot at God's theme park. The Bakkers were using donor money to provide themselves with a luxurious lifestyle, including opulent homes and expensive cars. Accounting practices within the ministry itself were sketchy. Cynical onlookers began to refer to PTL as "Pass the Loot."

The dam broke for the Bakkers in 1987 when Jessica Hahn, a former church secretary, came forward with accusations that Jim Bakker had sexually assaulted her in a hotel room several years earlier. PTL had been paying her hush money to keep the scandal hidden. PTL eventually went bankrupt in the wake of these cascading scandals, and Hahn was ordered to repay the money.

Jim Bakker's *coup de grace* came when prosecutors charged him with overselling lifetime memberships in Heritage USA's hotels. There just weren't enough hotel rooms to accommodate all the guests who paid into the program – and yet Bakker kept selling the memberships. At trial he was convicted of mail and wire fraud and sentenced to 45 years in prison. On appeal his prison term was greatly reduced, and Bakker is now a free man. He's back on TV spreading the gospel (i.e., hawking survivalist meal kits and other swag to the faithful).

Dipsh*t analytics for the bamboozling Bakkers:

- **Behavior:** chronic
- **Situation:** frenetic (The cost of their television broadcast operation combined with the financial burden of building and operating a theme park made PTL and Heritage USA

a money pit for the Bakkers. Their need for constant cash-flow probably explains Jim Bakker's overselling of hotel memberships.)

- **Cause:** Self-induced
- **Outcome:** 5 (destructive) for the Bakkers; 4 (damaging) for employees of PTL and Heritage USA, who lost their jobs when the Bakkers' house of cards collapsed; 4 (damaging) for people who bought Heritage USA memberships at substantial cost and for those who donated substantial sums to PTL; 4 (damaging) for creditors caught up in Heritage USA's bankruptcy; 2 (imposing) for investigators, prosecutors, and courts (criminal and bankruptcy).

A tsunami of scandals has also dogged several lesser and generally more buffoonish televangelists. One of the most mocked is the late faith healer, Rev. Ernest Angley. Known for his squat physique, absurd toupee, and creepy voice, Ohio-based Angley carried his faith healing schtick to nations far and wide. This got him arrested in Germany for "practicing therapy without a license."

According to the *Akron Beacon Journal,* which reportedly has an audio recording as proof, "in 1996…Ernest Angley admitted to his assistant minister that he had had sexual relations with a man who was employed by their church, Grace Cathedral in Cuyahoga Falls." In 2020 the church settled a lawsuit brought by a former minister, Brock Miller, who claimed that Angley examined his genitals and pressured him to get a vasectomy. Angley's ministry also had a for-profit restaurant adjacent to the sanctuary and used church members as volunteer labor. In 2012, a federal judge ordered the church to pay back wages and monetary damages to workers improperly classified as volunteers.

Angley died in 2021 at age 99. By the time the Brock Miller scandal was settled in 2020, Angley was a doddering old man within a year of his death. So he managed to hang on to his ministry until the end, surviving multiple scandals, of which those related here are but a few.

Dipsh*t analytics for Ernest Not Exactly Angel-y:

- **Behavior:** chronic
- **Situation:** benign
- **Cause:** habitual
- **Outcome:** 4 (damaging) for Angley who had to deal with these scandals and pay various judgments and settlements, but kept his ministry; 4 (damaging) for Brock Miller and anyone else who may have been exploited by Angley; 4 (damaging) for members of Angley's church or donors to his ministry who were adversely affected spiritually, psychologically, or financially; 2 (imposing) for investigators and courts.

One of the most unlikely implosions of a TV ministry was that of Robert Schuller. A Sunday morning staple during the late 20th century, Schuller's "Hour of Power" was broadcast from the magnificent Crystal Cathedral in Garden Grove, California. Congregants and TV viewers were welcomed with resonating pipe organ music and dramatic dancing fountains. Schuller was the thinking person's televangelist. He appeared in a clerical robe, and his messages combined biblical themes with pop psychology and self-help advice.

In the early 2000s Schuller stepped down from preaching and turned the pulpit over to his son, Robert A. Schuller. However, the elder Schuller remained on the board as did Bob Jr.'s sisters. Factions among the family soon emerged. Daddy Schuller clashed with Junior over his preaching and leadership, and so did the sisters. Meanwhile, the ministry struggled financially, due in part to extravagant spending. Declining membership ultimately made these problems insurmountable.

Unable to pay its $36 million mortgage and $7.5 million in other debts, the Crystal Cathedral filed for bankruptcy in 2010. Schuller's magisterial temple was put up for auction. In 2013 the Catholic Diocese bought the Crystal Cathedral out of bankruptcy.

I attended a Sunday service at the Crystal Cathedral back in the 1980s in the company of a local family who were generous donors to the church. In fact, Schuller recognized and greeted the father of this family from the pulpit, on live television. Afterwards, we were among a small group of supporters invited into the private areas of the building to enjoy a catered lunch. During this meal I got an up-close look at Robert Schuller as he was in real life and not as he presented himself on television. I found him to be a cold and aloof man, bordering on arrogant. Toward the end of the meal, he got up before everyone else, made no parting remarks, and drove away in his Cadillac.

Congregants attending services at the Crystal Cathedral passed a gift shop as they entered and exited. (Not exactly "exit through the gift shop," but close enough.) The store sold Schuller's books, of course, and tacky religious knick-knacks. What would Jesus buy?

Gift shop aside, Schuller's ministry stood head and shoulders above those of cartoonish figures like Ernest Angley or crass megachurch potentates like Ted Haggard. Financial mismanagement and intra-family power struggles facilitated the fall of the House of Schuller.

Dipsh*t analytics for the Crystal Clergyman:

- **Behavior:** occasional (Schuller built a fantastically successful ministry over several decades but lost it through boardroom intrigue – his one area of haplessness.)
- **Situation:** provocative (We can't know how to apportion blame for the Schuller family's in-fighting. For all we know, the situation could have been benign until one of them fomented the drama – or they could all be culpable. But once the squabbling started, the situation became provocative. And we do know that finances were a dire concern.)
- **Cause:** triggered
- **Outcome:** 5 (destructive) for the Schullers, their employees, and the ministry itself; 4 or 5 (damaging or destructive) for the ministry's creditors, depending on their financial losses; (3) disruptive for Crystal Cathedral members; (2) imposing for the bankruptcy court.

Existential Dread

What dark drives and impulses caused these once-powerful and ostensibly moral leaders to make such foolish choices – sex and drugs for Haggard, sexual abuse and labor violations for Angley, and a family-dominated, dysfunctional, spendthrift board for Schuller? Haggard and Angley obviously had same-sex attraction, but this only raises further questions: Why choose a theology that is anathema to who you are? Why train for a profession which expects you to rail against those like you who have homosexual attraction? Why deny your own nature? These are fascinating questions for a psychologist and would merit their own book.

Schuller wasn't brought down by a sex and drugs scandal, but rather by his own management and leadership failures. As soon as Schuller retired and appointed his son as minister, things began to unravel. This suggests a lack of insight and forethought. The overspending likely preceded the senior Schuller's abdication, which means he led those decisions as well.

As long as Daddy Schuller ruled supreme, the Crystal Cathedral managed to remain operational. But without him atop the ecclesiastical hierarchy, factions began jostling for control. It's especially tragic that this power struggle pitted siblings against each other. Schuller never should have allowed the board to be dominated by family members.

Existential theory may shed some light on the self-defeating behavior of these calamitous clergymen. We all may go through phases when we question our purpose in life and the meaning of life itself. During such times, we're likely to ponder the nature of existence and whether human values have any significance. This kind of alienation from ourselves, from society, and from moral grounding may lead us to seek out new experiences – even those that are risky, immoral, or out of character for us.

This sense of disconnectedness could explain Haggard's sexual adventurism, drug use, and feelings of invincibility as reported by one of his victims. The same could apply to Angley's sexual advances, but not so much to Schuller's flawed management. Haggard and Angley both worked in high-pressure, publicly visible ministries which placed severe constraints on their lifestyle choices. Underneath their holy façade, they had repressed drives and urges which probably made them feel confined, deprived, and frustrated. Forced to hide and deny their human nature for so long, they finally gave way to reckless adventurism.

As for Schuller's ministerial missteps, a better theory is psychologist Howard Gardner's *theory of multiple intelligences*. Intelligence is not a fixed trait, but rather a fluid and evolving talent. Gardner theorized that there are many kinds of intelligences. For example, I once had a girlfriend who was dyslexic. It was painful to watch her trying to read. But she could eyeball a room, cut wallpaper to size without measuring, and hang it flawlessly. With three graduate degrees and a lifetime of experience, I can't duplicate that skill. She and I are intelligent in different ways.

Schuller's intelligence was obvious in his ability to build a nationally respected ministry, in his ability to promote himself and his books, and in his conception of a visually inspiring place of worship. But he did not see the risk of allowing his family members to dominate the board of directors. And the church's overspending showed that he would not or could not adapt to declining cash flows. Like my ex-girlfriend, he could hang the wallpaper, but he couldn't read the handwriting on the wall.

The Dunning-Kruger effect, as you'll recall, describes the tendency of uninformed or incompetent people to overestimate their skill and ability. When smart, competent people make the same judgment error, it's called the *overconfidence effect.* Intelligent and highly successful people are prone to assuming that their knowledge and experience in certain areas will be just as effective in other areas. For example, Schuller's success in building the Crystal Cathedral into a multi-million-dollar ministry didn't carry over into governance and financial matters – at least not when those issues threatened to bring down everything he worked for. Similarly, if Haggard felt invincible as his victim alleged, this too could signal that the profligate pastor fell victim to the overconfidence effect.

If these televangelist cases tell us anything, it's that intelligence does not guarantee wise decisions in all circumstances, nor do talent, knowledge, and experience act as an absolute preventative against dipsh*t behavior. Remember Richard Kazmeier, the biology professor who smuggled wildlife specimens into the United States in violation of the Lacey Act? He imported at least 358 "skulls, skeletons, and taxidermy mounts" without declaring them, although customs officers had caught him at least three times and allowed him to file paperwork retroactively. Kazmeier drew a prison sentence and hefty fine. He's another brilliant man who made hundreds of ill-fated decisions.

A final concept that can help explain the personal failures of these formerly prominent preachers is *self-control depletion theory* (also called *ego depletion theory*). Research by psychologists Roy F. Baumeister and Diane M. Tice suggests that self-control is a finite resource that can be exhausted under prolonged exertion of willpower. Engaging in tasks that require self-restraint or decision-making can make subsequent acts of self-discipline more difficult. This depletion can lead to a decreased ability to resist impulses, make rational choices, or exert willpower. The heavy responsibility that fell daily upon the shoulders of these religious leaders may have impaired their ability to resist temptation. Depletion may have led them to make snap decisions and to fall back on heuristics and schemas in situations that required more discretion and deliberation.

Passion Plays

Pastoral peccadilloes don't just happen at the highest levels of evangelism. A few priests and preachers in your own community may be perpetrating sordid schemes. But as the good book says, "he that troubleth his own house shall inherit the wind." Or as we would say today, "what goes around, comes around." Take a look at what these saintly sinners have inherited.

Heaven with a Gun. Police were summoned to a hotel in McComb, Mississippi where they found that Pastor Randy Prenell, Jr., age 25, had shot his wife, Gabrielle Prenell, and then turned the gun on himself. Mrs. Prenell sustained wounds in the arm and abdomen, and the good reverend suffered a self-administered stomach wound. Both survived. The pistol-packing preacher man faces charges of domestic assault.

Prenell is pastor of the Bright Morning Star Missionary Baptist Church of Pineville, Louisiana (though perhaps for not much longer). He's held that position for about a year. Previously he was a deputy sheriff. In an April, 2023 Facebook post, Prenell wrote, "At the age of 25, I often hear that I'm far beyond my years. However, I never get satisfied with where I am…I'm constantly looking for more." Earlier, he referred to his wife as "the woman that I love and owe my life to."

But let's hear from Mrs. Prenell. According to KALB-TV, she filed for a protective order against him in 2016. In her petition, "she detailed instances where Prenell was violent with her, saying 'I've been constantly getting beaten by my husband and I fear for the life of myself and my unborn child.' She goes on to say that Prenell often pointed guns and threatened to kill her."

Call me unreasonable, but I'm not sure this man should be trusted with either a badge or a pulpit.

The investigation is ongoing as of this writing. Authorities say it's possible Prenell may face additional charges. No motive for the shooting has been revealed. It looks like the Prenells will get a chance to present their personal testimonies – not in church, but in court.

Dipsh*t analytics for the Randy "Glock of Ages" Prenell:

- **Behavior:** chronic
- **Situation:** frenetic or provocative (We don't know the motive or what led up to the shooting. The situation even could have been benign until Prenell started something. But I'm assuming fraught circumstances.)
- **Cause:** habitual (Prenell could have been triggered by something his wife said or did, but given his alleged history of domestic violence, I'm assuming an aggressive and volatile personality).

- **Outcome:** 5 (destructive) for both Prenells; 3 (disruptive) for the hotel and other guests; 4 (damaging) for the church and its members who must now decide what to do about Prenell and find a way to restore serenity to the congregation; 2 (imposing) for the police, prosecutor, and court.

The Gift of Grab. James Gill, age 81, served as senior pastor of Liberty Baptist Church in Gallatin, Tennessee until his recent retirement. Gill was also the director of a local food bank. But now the octogenarian stands accused of allegedly stealing over $250,000 of the food bank's money. A news release issued by the district attorney's office stated:

> James Gill (DOB: 6/1/42), who was employed as the director of the Sumner County Food Bank, used the organization's money to make personal purchases. He also wrote checks to himself and others from the food bank's account and transferred the money to other accounts under a different non-profit name. Further investigation revealed that Gill paid a food bank volunteer for sex acts.

Gill is charged with theft, money laundering, and prostitution. The food bank continues to operate under the auspices of a different church. It reportedly serves up to 1,000 families each week.

Dipsh*t analytics for the allegedly pilfering preacher:

- **Behavior:** chronic (He could be a hybrid, but when we're not sure, we assume chronic.)
- **Situation:** benign (Most likely, the money and the sexually alluring volunteer were minding their own business.)
- **Cause:** self-induced

- **Outcome:** 5 (destructive) for Gill. Even if he's found not guilty, he'll never live down the humiliation of these charges – and if he's guilty, he will be ordered to make restitution and possibly get jail time, even at his age; 4 (damaging) for the food bank; (3) disruptive for his former church; 0 (null) for families receiving food assistance, since another church has stepped in to keep the food bank operational.

Won't the Altar Boys Be Jealous. A now-defrocked Catholic priest in Louisiana has pleaded guilty to one felony count of obscenity. Travis Clark, age 39, got caught recording a sex tape featuring himself and two dominatrices atop the altar of his Pearl River church. The archdiocese was not amused (aroused maybe, but not amused). The altar was deemed desecrated and had to be destroyed. It was consigned to the purifying flames of a bonfire.

In return for his guilty plea, Clark received a three-year suspended sentence and a $1,000 fine. He also paid $8,000 in restitution to the church. The two ladies of convenience got off a bit easier. They were allowed to plead guilty to a misdemeanor charge of vandalism, for which they received a two-year suspended sentence. It's getting so a priest can't even blow off a little steam without the church and criminal court meddling in his affairs.

Dipsh*t analytics for this unholy trysting trinity:

- **Behavior:** chronic
- **Situation:** benign (The altar probably wasn't flirting with them.)
- **Cause:** self-induced

- **Outcome:** 5 (destructive) for Clark since it cost him several thousand dollars, his priesthood, and his dignity; 4 (damaging) for the frolicking floozies; 3 (disruptive) for the church and archdiocese; 2 (imposing) for the police, prosecutor, and court.

Suffer the Children. Carl Matthew Johnson, age 78, will probably spend the rest of his life in prison. What a come-down for the former mayor of West Bountiful, Utah and Mormon bishop. Four women tearfully testified how Johnson molested them over several years spanning the 1980s and 1990s. Some of the abuse even happened while he was mayor, but no allegations date back to the 1970s when he was a bishop in the Church of Jesus Christ of Latter-Day Saints. As *The Salt Lake Tribune* put it, "Prosecutor Adam Blanch called Johnson a 'wolf in sheep's clothing' who manipulated and tricked his church, community, family and friends so he could be protected and could live 'in bliss.'"

Johnson received an open-ended sentence with a minimum of ten years to serve. Several character witnesses urged the court to consider Johnson's decades of service to the community and the church. Judge David J. Williams brushed those pleas aside, saying no quantity of good deeds could atone for the lasting harm Johnson caused. The judge also noted the duration of the crime and Johnson's history of concealing it.

Dipsh*t analytics for the Mormon molester:

- **Behavior:** chronic (He could be classified as a hybrid type, since his sex crimes seem to be the only area of his life that

148

qualifies as dipsh*ttery. But given that he led a double life to enable his predatory behavior, I'm going with chronic.)

- **Situation:** benign (No external factors prodded him into criminal molestation.)
- **Cause:** self-induced
- **Outcome:** 5 (destructive) for Johnson, his family, his victims, and their families; 2 (imposing) for the police, prosecutor, and court.

One of Johnson's victims said she often asks herself, "How could someone who was a Latter-Day Saint bishop do this? How could a mayor do this?" Her inability to comprehend relentlessly callous and evil actions is understandable. "Because he could" may be the answer, but it's not a satisfying one. There are some theories that can help us untangle this knotty problem, however.

A "golden oldie" is Freud's *psychodynamic theory* which forms the basis of psychoanalysis. Because of advances in psychological research and neuroscience, much of Freud's work has been discredited. But certainly not all of it.

Freud conceptualized the mind as consisting of the id, the ego, and the superego, roughly corresponding to the triune brain structure. The id corresponds to the reptilian brain (impulsive, selfish, amoral). Acting in opposition to these dark urges is the neomammalian superego, which is moralistic and judgmental. Mediating between these conflicting drives is the paleomammalian ego, our shrewd and pragmatic mind.

It's not difficult to imagine how the ego of a Mormon bishop – someone constantly scrutinized and expected to be pious and upright – could become exhausted and ineffective in mediating between his frustrated sexual desires on the one hand and the church's restrictive moral expectations on the other. The same psychodynamic conflict could explain the dipsh*ttery of Ted Haggard, Ernest Angley, James Gill, or Travis Clark.

Another risk for people in prominent or highly successful positions is selective morality. *Moral disengagement theory*, developed by psychologist Albert Bandura, proposes that when people want to commit acts they would normally consider wrong, they're likely to rationalize and make excuses for their unethical behavior. They do this by mentally disengaging from their moral standards and suppressing their feelings of guilt. In other words, they deliberately "hit the snooze button" on their superego/neomammalian mind, so that their id/reptilian brain can have its way. Positions of power can trigger moral disengagement and cause leaders to feel that the rules no longer apply to them.

Morally disengaged people have several mental machinations they can exploit to facilitate their nefarious behavior. They may use *moral justification* to rationalize and twist logic. For example, a married preacher trying to seduce a female church member might argue that his marriage is a sham because his wife has lost her faith, but that he and his prospective paramour share a sacred love in the eyes of God.

Another familiar tactic of the morally compromised is *euphemistic labeling* – using verbiage to frame a dubious activity as benign or benevolent. Ernest Angley reportedly got a young man, who was about to be married, to expose his genitals under the guise of giving pre-marital counseling. Another slippery tactic is *advantageous comparison*, a way to make offensive behavior seem not so bad by comparing it to something similar, but worse. Suppose a philandering reverend got caught cheating. He might compare himself to King David, who lusted after Bathsheba and contrived to have her husband killed in battle so he could have her. If David, a great hero of the Bible, could order someone's murder and still serve God, then the minister might argue that his own infidelity is no big deal.

Displacement of responsibility is another familiar tactic. In the biblical story of Adam and Eve, he sampled the forbidden fruit after she persuaded him. When God came calling, Adam blamed Eve for tempting him. But they both knew the tree was off-limits, so Adam's craven attempt to shift the blame didn't work.

Dissolution of responsibility is similar, but instead of blaming a person, the morally disengaged person blames a group. As details about Jim Bakker's financial grifting at PTL and Heritage USA began to leak out, news media began reporting the shocking allegations. The Bakkers went into attack mode, using their PTL broadcast to blame Satan and the media for their troubles. As the Bakkers would have it, their ministry was squeaky clean, but the devil was using secular media to persecute them.

One final tactic used by the morally disengaged to avoid cognitive dissonance, guilt, and hesitation about doing harm is *dehumanization.* When right-wing preachers picket gay pride events and hurl vile insults at participants, they usually claim that the Bible commands them to preach to the unsaved. This allows them to shout slurs at people they despise while claiming a biblical imperative for themselves. And by dehumanizing gays as hell-bound sinners, they can rationalize their hate speech as "preaching."

A Wing and a Prayer

This chapter has relied heavily on ordained offenders to prove that whom the gods wish to destroy, they first make a dipsh*t. Perhaps it is fitting therefore to conclude with a parable. The one I have in mind is not from the Bible, but from Greek myth. It's the story of Daedalus and his son, Icarus.

King Minos imprisoned the father and son in his labyrinth, a maze originally built to confine the terrible Minotaur (slain by Theseus), but now used as a prison. Daedalus collected feathers and bits of wax, and when he had enough, he made wings for himself and Icarus. They would escape the labyrinth by flying out of it.

On the day they were ready to make their flight to freedom, Daedalus warned Icarus against flying too low, because moisture from the sea would penetrate his wings, making them too heavy. And, he also cautioned his son about flying too high, as the sun could melt the wax holding the wings together. Take a middle path, neither too high nor too low, Daedalus instructed.

Ancient myths usually included a moral or even a warning. The tale of Daedalus and Icarus cautions us not to choose the path of too little or too much in life, but rather a middle course of moderation. Just as the sea mist would have saturated Icarus' wings, some churches burden their members and ministers with puritanical standards of behavior that put them under enormous pressure. Then, when living a life of self-abnegation becomes un-sustainable, congregants and clergy alike may react by flying too close to the sun. They may resort to reckless, self-destructive, and even criminal behavior as the cases in this chapter have shown. Such are the circumstances from which dipsh*ts readily emerge.

We're not plaster saints. Moderation allows us to live like human beings. We have a paleomammalian ego for a reason – to mediate between reckless impulses and impossibly restrictive moral standards.

Finally, I offer this piece of advice which I hope you'll remember even if you learn nothing else from this chapter: Beware of any faith healer wearing a bad toupee. Baldy, heal thyself!

* * *

"If stupidity got us into this mess, then why can't it get us out?"
– Will Rogers

Chapter Eight

The Seventh Law: Do Not Attribute to Malice That Which Can be Explained by Dipsh*ttery Alone

An outdoor shopping mall in Beavercreek, Ohio organized an elaborate Easter egg hunt for the community in April 2023. Hundreds of eggs were hidden, and prizes were to be given away as well. This was the second annual Easter event sponsored by the mall, and it was presumed to herald an ongoing springtime tradition. But alas, this was not to be. On the day after the event, the mall posted a blistering Facebook message condemning the participants and vowing never to host another Easter egg hunt. What on earth could have gone so terribly wrong at such a wholesome event?

Before the hunt, organizers gave instructions to the parents and older children as follows: First, there would be a brief hunt only for one- and two-year-olds. These toddlers would search in a small area designated just for them. Next, the main egg hunt would begin with three- and four-year-olds getting a 60 second head start. After this, all children could join in. Adults were not allowed to pick up eggs. Clear enough, right?

When the "Go!" command was given, all instructions went by the wayside. Children of all ages and their parents rushed onto the field. Adults began scooping up eggs intended for kids, and the mall later stated that "We saw grown adults pushing children out of the way, and people getting knocked over." Many parents probably would have obeyed the rules under normal circumstances, but when chaos ensued, they joined in so that their kids at least had a chance to participate. It was bedlam.

Over 2,000 eggs had been hidden, but many children left the event empty-handed while others (and many adults) went home with an abundance. Not holding back their anger, the mall's management said in their Facebook post:

> Our staff dedicated 2 months to preparing for this event, and we had 10 staff members and a softball team of 12 girls volunteer their time yesterday to help run our event – everyone was very upset with the outcome of the Egg Hunt, and the way they were treated by community members at the conclusion of the event.

And that's the way it goes – egg hunt with dipsh*ts and end up with egg on your face. (This being America, I suppose it's a "win" that no one fired an assault weapon during the festivities.)

The phrase, "Never attribute to malice that which is adequately explained by stupidity" first appeared in Arthur Block's *Murphy's Law Book Two: More Reasons Why Things Go Wrong!* (where it's called "Hanlon's Razor" after Robert J. Hanlon). Similar thoughts also appear in the writings of H. G. Wells and Johann Wolfgang von Goethe. Robert A. Heinlein warned against attributing events "to villainy that simply result from stupidity" in his *Logic of Empire*. Similarly, Winston Churchill suggested that Charles De Gaulle's obstinance toward his British allies in World War II "may be founded on stupidity rather than malice."

The seventh law, "Do not attribute to malice that which can be explained by dipsh*ttery alone," aligns quite well with Hanlon's Razor. Hanlon addressed only stupidity while the seventh law encompasses behavior that is both stupid and despicable. There's bound to be much overlap between these two pearls of wisdom. Henceforth, I propose that the seventh law be known as "Hartley's Purloined Razor" (accept no substitutes), with a tip of the hat to Hanlon for his prescience.

As this is being written, the implosion of the Titan submersible, resulting in the death of all those aboard, is in the news. The undersea vehicle took adventurers to see the wreck of the Titanic at a cost of $250,000 per passenger. Stockton Rush, the CEO and co-founder of the company that developed the Titan was on board and is among the dead.

A few years earlier, Rush's company, OceanGate Expeditions, hired safety expert Karl Stanley to study and monitor the vehicle's experimental design. During a test run off the Bahamas in 2019, Stanley says he became alarmed when he heard loud noises during the voyage. Afterwards, he notified Rush, stating "From the intensity of the sounds, the fact that they never totally stopped at depth, and the fact that there were sounds at about 300 feet that indicated a relaxing of stored energy…would indicate that there is an area of the hull that is breaking down," according to an email quoted by CNN. Rush reportedly never responded to Stanley's warning.

The company received separate warnings from its own director of marine operations, David Lochridge, who feared that the sub's hull monitoring system was inadequate, because it would warn of impending doom "milliseconds before an implosion." Rather than fixing that issue, OceanGate fired Lochridge. Meanwhile, Rush told one prospective adventurer that the submersible was "safer than scuba diving," HuffPost reported.

Rush seems to have been in denial about the risks. He reminds me of the mayor in *Jaws* who wouldn't believe that a shark attack had occurred and insisted that the beaches remain open. Rush may have fallen victim to the *Pollyanna syndrome*, a cognitive bias which predisposes a person to block out negative information and to take only the most optimistic view. (Pollyanna is the title character of a 1913 novel about a girl who insists on looking only on the bright side of life.) *Confirmation bias* is a similar thinking error which may have affected Rush. It causes people to accept facts which support their preconceived notions and to reject contrary evidence. He obviously believed his own faulty conclusions, since he bet his life on the Titan's seaworthiness. In this case there was no malice in sending people to the ocean floor aboard the fatally flawed submersible – it was pure, unmitigated dipsh*ttery.

Dipsh*t analytics for Stockton Rush-to-Destruction:

- **Behavior:** chronic (An argument could be made that he was a hybrid type, since he was a successful corporate executive and we have no other indication of persistent dipsh*ttery. But that's exactly the problem: We know nothing else about him, and his unwillingness to heed warnings from experts tips the scale to chronic.)

- **Situation:** provocative (Rush was dealing with doubts and criticisms from multiple sources, and his responses ranged from ignoring them to firing the messenger.)
- **Cause:** self-induced. (Certainly, his reactions were triggered by unwelcome advice and warnings, but it is his own stubbornness and willful blindness that enabled the ensuing disaster.)
- **Outcome:** 5 (destructive) for Rush, the other passengers on the Titan, their families, and the company; 3 (disruptive) for the Coast Guard and any other rescuers or recovery specialists. (This bizarre crisis has been a boon for news media, however.)

Here are more examples of individuals creating controversy, chaos, or confusion – not by malice, but by their obtuse, obnoxious behavior. None of these can match the epic tragedy or high drama of the Titan implosion, but they are more representative of real-life dipsh*t behavior.

Tie One On. A motorist in Texas called the Archer County Sheriff's Office and asked that someone investigate a woman dragging a child alongside a vehicle. A deputy was dispatched and soon located the vehicle in question. The driver, Mary Luise Stade, age 61, told the deputy that her son had insulted her and that she pulled over and refused to continue until he apologized. She denied anything more than that, and the officer let her go.

Meanwhile, the sheriff received a text from another motorist which included a video of the boy being dragged beside the car. Stade reportedly used a seatbelt to somehow strap the boy outside the vehicle. The video showed Stade starting and stopping abruptly, with the boy forced to run alongside. The Law & Crime website reported that "the child can be seen clinging to the side of the vehicle with both of his feet lifted up off of the ground as the car continues to move forward." The child's age has not been revealed, but these circumstances suggest a pre-teen.

The deputy was dispatched again to apprehend Stade. This time she reportedly told him that the boy was out of control, and she was merely trying to discipline him. Incredibly, the deputy let her go again. But later that day, deputies arrested her in another county and charged her with child endangerment. Charging documents filed with the court state that Stade "placed the child in imminent danger of death or serious bodily injury."

Unless Stade's son is adopted, I have questions about a 61-year-old woman with a pre-teen son. But that aside, it doesn't appear that Stade was hellbent on killing or permanently maiming him. If that were the case, she probably wouldn't have done it on a public highway in view of multiple witnesses. Most likely, the boy had gotten on her last nerve. There probably was no more malice in Stade's actions than in those of parents who beat the snot out of their kids in Walmart. It's stupid and cruel but motivated by righteous intentions rather than malice. Dipsh*ttery alone is sufficient to account for Stade's rage-filled retaliation.

Dipsh*t analytics for Stade's alleged roadway discipline:

- **Behavior:** chronic
- **Situation:** provocative
- **Cause:** triggered

- **Outcome:** 5 (destructive) for Stade, who now faces criminal charges and may be at risk for losing custody; 4 (damaging) for the kid, who presumably wasn't seriously injured but must live with this experience; 2 (imposing) for law officers, the prosecutor, the court, and for witnesses who made reports.

Hell House. See if you can spot the demons in this story. Andrew Hartzler, age 25, who was raised in a fundamentalist Christian family, no longer speaks to his parents. "I told them you chose your religion over your son...goodbye," he said in a TikTok video.

Hartzler recounted how he came out as gay to his parents at age 14. They tried to "cure" their son by sending him to a gay conversion camp. Afterwards, they made him see a conversion counselor three times a week throughout his high school years.

Parental intervention didn't stop after high school. Hartzler said that his parents enrolled him at Oral Roberts University (ORU) in the belief that he would be isolated from gays at the ultra-Christian school. On the contrary, he met other homosexual classmates who were sent there for the same reason. During his sophomore year, Hartzler told his parents emphatically that he was gay, that the conversion therapy didn't work, and that he was no longer going to pretend otherwise. And so his parents upped the ante: They called in an exorcist, he said.

Suspecting that his parents might be going through his possessions while he was away at ORU, Hartzler said that he installed hidden cameras in his room. When he checked the video feed on his app, he saw the ersatz exorcist walking around his room saying,

"Devil to go in Jesus' name, you foul spirit, you leave. Every evil spirit go now in Jesus' name. Something foul is happening in this closet in Jesus' name. Every evil spirit go now in Jesus' name."

I have questions. Did the devil ever leave Andrew Hartzler's room and venture into other parts of the home? If so, why wasn't anyone else demonically infused with the spirit of gayness? And if not, what kept the evil spirit confined to that one room? What if the demon was no longer in that bedroom at the time of exorcism? What if it had moved with Hartzler to ORU? If "Devil to go in Jesus' name" is all that's needed to banish the demons of gayness, why hasn't all the gay been prayed away long ago? When are they going to get around to exorcizing the demons of dipsh*ttery, which seem to haunt the rest of that household?

This case differs from the others I've presented, because there is no crime or newsworthy confrontation. It's a young man's account of problems within his family. I believe Andrew Hartzler's account of familial religious fanaticism. But the fact remains that I only have one side of the story. He's chosen to go public with this, but his parents have not. Even though they sound reprehensible based on his revelations, I won't apply dipsh*t analytics to them. Nevertheless, it's a good example of how interventions by ill-informed people can harm others despite no malicious intent.

Police Farce. Shortly before midnight on April 5 2023, three police officers in Farmington, New Mexico were dispatched to investigate a domestic disturbance. The dispatcher provided them with the correct street address as well as a photo of the house. The street was dark when the officers arrived, and somehow they went to the wrong residence.

Bodycam video showed that the officers knocked and announced themselves three times. No one came to the door. An officer checked with the dispatcher again and was given the correct address once more. It appears that the officers then realized they were at the wrong house.

As the cops were about to leave, the front door opened and the resident, Robert Dotson, age 52, appeared, holding a gun. All three officers opened fire without any warning, killing Dotson on the spot. His wife then picked up the gun and fired but stopped when she realized the men outside were police. She was not harmed nor was she charged. Besides the couple, there were two children in the residence.

The video is unsteady, and the shooting happened within seconds after Dotson opened the door, so it's unclear whether the victim was pointing the gun at police or merely holding it. The Dotson family's lawyer said that a freeze-frame video capture proves that Dotson had the weapon pointed toward the ground and not at officers.

These officers had the correct address (confirmed twice) as well as a picture of the house. Even so, they went to the wrong residence. When the homeowner opened the door, they fired as soon as they saw the gun without identifying themselves as police or giving any warning. No one had malicious intent, but a man is dead, his wife is a widow, and two fatherless children must live with the memory of being awakened to the shooting death of their dad – the result of a stupid and despicable set of circumstances.

Dipsh*t analytics for the Farmington Firing Squad:

- **Behavior:** occasional (The officers were experienced and presumably in good standing with the department. This seems to have been a bizarre incident and out-of-character for these men.)
- **Situation:** frenetic (A domestic violence call means a confrontational situation. However, the situation wasn't provocative until the shooting started.)
- **Cause:** triggered (Literally.)
- **Outcome:** 5 (destructive) for the Dotsons; 4 or 5 (damaging or destructive) for the officers, depending on whether they are cleared or found liable; 3 (disruptive) for the police department; 2 (imposing) for investigators and the court.

Disciple of Heist. An Alabama church went broke and had to shut down after it was discovered that their secretary had stolen over $89,000. The crime was exposed when a $75 check bounced due to insufficient funds. Carmen Ramer Davis, age 59, pleaded guilty to eight counts of wire fraud and received an 18-month sentence. The court also ordered her to make restitution.

Incredibly, Davis embezzled from the Brooklyn Congregational Methodist Church for over a decade with no one becoming suspicious. In addition to writing unauthorized checks, she secretly obtained a debit card and used it to withdraw cash from ATMs. She reportedly gambled with much of the money at casinos in Alabama and Mississippi. (The rest she just wasted on living expenses.)

Now, it's obvious that theft requires malicious intent to commit a crime. Davis's embezzlement cannot be explained by dipsh*ttery alone (but neither is it excluded). It's the unfathomable blindness of church leaders that deserves attention in this case. These people were not malicious – in fact, quite the opposite. But they allowed one person to have control of the church's funds with no meaningful oversight or verification of financial transactions. Their lax approach to finances allowed Davis to steal for many years. By the time they noticed a problem, the church was flat broke. In the immortal words of Forrest Gump, "Stupid is as stupid does."

Dipsh*t analytics for the Alabama church chuckleheads:

- **Behavior:** chronic (The church's leaders may have been competent individuals in all areas of their lives except this one, which would make them hybrid types. But since we don't know, we go with our default rating.)
- **Situation:** benign. (They didn't see any problems and apparently didn't look for any.)
- **Cause:** habitual (Ten years of "just trust the secretary.")
- **Outcome:** 5 (destructive) for the church, its minister, and its congregation as well as for Davis and her family; 2 (imposing) for the police, prosecutor, and court.

They say that "the road to hell is paved with good intentions." I know that road. It passes through Dipsh*tville. The above cases show that ignorance, incompetence, and good (yet obtuse) intentions can be just as destructive as malicious malfeasance. Now let's explore why.

When the Brain Takes a Holiday

Sometimes our brains go on vacation without us. They take a luxury cruise down a river called "Denial." Or when they prefer a "staycation," they close themselves off rather than exploring and inquiring. At other times, they take off on a spontaneous adventure that ends with a shout of, "Hold my beer!" In more mundane terms, our brains occasionally deny obvious risks, fail to consider all the evidence, or jump to conclusions. You already know about heuristics and schemas and how they sometimes can fail us. Now we'll look at other reasons why our brains occasionally go on holiday.

Did you know that knee-jerk reactions and jumping to conclusions are among the ways the brain manages stress? Those aren't the best ways, and certainly we shouldn't go off half-cocked just because that might make us feel better. Our neomammalian brains need to regulate hair-trigger responses.

Emotional regulation theory proposes two ways to control emotional, hyper-reactive impulses. The first is an *antecedent-focused* approach, which just means either re-evaluating the situation or changing external circumstances so that there's no longer a need to react. Then there's a *response-focused* alternative which means drawing upon experience, judgment, and critical-thinking skills to respond in a way that's proportionate to the situation.

The Farmington cops apparently fired at Robert Dotson the instant they saw he had a gun, without identifying themselves and ordering him to drop it. Mary Luise Stade's alleged strapping of her son to the side of their car seems to have been the knee-jerk reaction of a mother at her wit's end. Inadequate emotional regulation using antecedent- or response-focused skills can create havoc even without malicious intent.

Quite another explanation is needed for Andrew Hartzler's parents who he says sent him to gay conversion therapy and hired an exorcist to de-demonize his room. *Attribution theory* provides the key to understanding their behavior. Developed by psychologist Fritz Heider in the 1950s, attribution theory holds that we attribute the causes of behavior to either internal factors or external factors. Whether we attribute someone's behavior to internal or external causes will affect our opinions about, and reactions to, that person. Our interpretations of later events involving that person will also be influenced.

For example, suppose I see someone speeding and weaving in and out of traffic on the highway. I might assume that the person is drunk, or on drugs, or just an arrogant jerk. In that case, I'd be casting blame on the driver. But what if the driver is a father trying to get his child to the emergency room because of a rattlesnake bite? That's an external or situational cause for his behavior. My assumptions about the driver would be wrong.

According to Hartzler, his parents couldn't accept that his homosexuality is an inherent trait. It must have come from the outside (i.e., demons). Their attribution of his sexual orientation to Satanic spirits poisoned their relationship with their son. It prompted them to send him to quack conversion therapy and then to engage the services of a Bible-thumping exorcist. Their attributions led to behavior so extreme and offensive that their son cut off contact with them.

Still another theory is needed to understand why church leaders would be so hands-off that they enabled an embezzler's crime spree for over ten years. Forensic accountants and other fraud-detection professionals use the *fraud triangle* to predict circumstances conducive to misappropriation. The triangle's three sides are *motivation*, *opportunity*, and *rationalization*.

If someone has the need or desire to steal and can justify the act to him- or herself, then the crime will probably be committed if there is an opportunity. Motivation and rationalization are inherent to the thief. Only the opportunity factor is external and within the control of the potential victim (e.g., employer, church, business partner, etc.). Naturally, fraud-prevention experts focus on implementing controls that minimize opportunities for fraud. Leaders of the Alabama church failed in their duty to restrict Davis's opportunities.

But the question remains, *Why be so lackadaisical about church finances?* No explanation from the church's minister or its governing body is available, but we can make some intelligent conjectures. One possible explanation is the *information asymmetry theory*. In 1970 George Akerlof, an economist, published a paper that explored risks in business transactions when one party has more relevant information than the other, such as when one is buying a used car from a private seller.

In a typical used car transaction, the seller will have more knowledge about the vehicle than the buyer. He or she may exploit this one-sided advantage to cheat the buyer. A prudent buyer will be aware of this asymmetry and remain skeptical about the seller's sales pitch. A rational buyer will factor this uncertainty into the maximum amount he or she is willing to pay.

In the Alabama church case, it's clear that Davis had asymmetrical information about the congregation's finances compared to the church's leaders. This shouldn't have been allowed, but it was. Davis provided the motivation and rationalization, and the church facilitated the opportunity. Add to this the prevalence of *trust-based belief formation* among members of the same faith, and a possible explanation comes into focus. Trust-based relationships, especially among members of a close-knit religious group, serve as the foundation for forming beliefs about each other's intentions, honesty, and reliability. It's circular reasoning: "*I trust members of my church, because they are members of my church and therefore trustworthy.*"

We know that "wherever you go, there you are." Unfortunately, our brains sometimes can be elsewhere. It's fine if our minds sometimes wander, just so long as they don't stumble off a cliff and land in Dipsh*t Canyon.

On Gullibility

A Canadian grandmother sits in a Hong Kong jail charged with drug trafficking after falling victim to a romance scam. This tragic trajectory of events began when Suzana Thayer sought companionship online following her husband's death. She corresponded with a man on Facebook who said his name was "James Caywood." The precise details are murky, but after chatting with her for a while, Caywood sent her a bogus marriage certificate "proving" that they were husband and wife. He also provided her with a plane ticket to Ethiopia, where Caywood said he would meet her.

Thayer swallowed this con hook, line, and sinker. She flew to Ethiopia, but – surprise! – Caywood wasn't there. Instead, she was met by a friend of Caywood's who said there had been a change of plans. Now Caywood would meet her in Hong Kong. Thayer received another plane ticket and a suitcase, supposedly a gift from Caywood. (I'll bet you're way ahead of me by now.)

The gullible grandmother arrived in Hong Kong expecting to meet her "husband." Customs inspectors found cocaine hidden in the garments in Thayer's suitcase. She had been duped into acting as an international drug mule. Authorities took her into custody at the airport.

Here's the kicker: This is second time Thayer fell victim to a romance scammer. The first time she lost $200,000 to a man claiming to be a physician in Syria. She wrote a book about this experience entitled, *I've Been Conned: A Book for Dummies.* (It's on Amazon if you're interested.) Incredibly, she didn't heed the expensive lessons of that debacle.

Sometimes naivety and gullibility can be innocent and charming, as when a child believes in the Tooth Fairy. More often, however, they're forms of stupidity. Just consider what Thayer's credulity did to both herself and her family. Leaving aside the $200,000 she lost, which could have benefitted her children and grandchildren, her family is now burdened with mobilizing governmental and legal resources to rescue their mother from her own disastrous choices. According to *Global News*, "Angela Thayer asked her mother not to go, but Suzana Thayer insisted she would not pass up an opportunity to travel, having never previously left Canada." Besides being gullible, she was also unwilling to heed prudent advice from a trustworthy source.

I reluctantly consider Thayer to be a dipsh*t. Yes, she was a victim (twice), and no one deserves what's happened to her. But her failure to heed obvious red flags or to learn from her previous victimization has caused her family enormous distress. I'm sure that being a prisoner in a Chinese jail is a horrendous experience for her. I'm not unsympathetic. But just as people with personality disorders don't get a free pass to cause distress to others, neither does being a naïve and heedless risk-taker. Despite her sad fate, I think Thayer's behavior was both stupid and despicable.

Dipsh*t analytics for the globe-trotting grandma:

- **Behavior:** chronic (Indubitably.)
- **Situation:** benign
- **Cause:** self-induced (Possibly habitual, but I'll assume the lesser evil.)
- **Outcome:** 5 (destructive) for Thayer and her family; 2 (imposing) for Chinese authorities and for Canadian governmental and legal authorities involved in her case.

Thayer's abortive attempts to find romance online apparently stemmed from grief and loneliness after her husband's death. This is quite understandable. Many psychological theories address our need for love and friendship. *Need for belongingness theory*, the by-product of several psychologists (one of them Abraham Maslow who developed the famous *hierarchy of needs*), delves into our dependence on relationships. The theory holds that this basic human need can be traced back to evolutionary biology. Our primitive ancestors who formed close personal and social bonds enjoyed more security and increased their chances of survival.

When we are deprived of companionship and connectedness, the theory notes that we may seek alternative means to fulfill that need. For example, we might engage in maladaptive behaviors, such as negative attention-seeking, and we may experience emotional distress. If we pursue new relationships in an inept or reckless manner, as Thayer did, we may suffer negative consequences.

Another example of non-malicious naivety is seen every year in American national parks, especially Yellowstone. Despite signs and warnings from park officials, tourists are frequently caught on video approaching bison, elk, and bears. They climb over barriers to walk on the brittle and unstable ground around boiling hot springs and geysers. There's even a phenomenon called "hot-potting," which has tourists venturing into prohibited areas of Yellowstone in search of a hot springs to soak in.

An Oregon man suffered an excruciating death in his quest for a hot-potting site. Colin Nathaniel Scott, age 23, went into an off-limits area with his sister looking for a suitable spring. His sister told park authorities that he leaned down to test the water temperature with his hand and fell headlong into scalding, acidic water. By the time rescuers arrived on the scene, there were no remains to recover. His body had dissolved in the boiling spring.

Like Thayer, Scott not only brought ruin to himself but grief to his family. They lost a son and brother prematurely because of his recklessness, and they don't even have a body to bury.

Dipsh*t analytics for scofflaw Scott:

- **Behavior:** chronic
- **Situation:** benign
- **Cause:** self-induced
- **Outcome:** 5 for Scott and his family; 3 (disruptive) for rescuers who had to attempt a recovery at substantial risk to themselves; 2 (imposing) for investigators.

Humans harbor many faults which can be destructive even in the absence of malicious intent. Some of these are denial, naivety, gullibility, incompetence, irresponsibility, recklessness, a paucity of common sense, failure to consider how one's behavior affects others, closed-mindedness, and willful ignorance. When a jilted lover slashes his or her ex-lover's tires, we understand that kind of malice. We don't condone it, but we comprehend it. Non-malicious mayhem, on the other hand, is frequently incomprehensible.

How do we make sense of a mother who straps her misbehaving kid to the outside of a car? What should we conclude about a CEO who not only ignores the experts who raised safety concerns about his experimental sub, but actually resents their interference? Why would a woman swindled out of a fortune by a romance scammer allow herself to be horrifically bamboozled again? These kinds of baffling questions in response to dumbfounding behavior indicate that dipsh*ttery, not malice, is afoot.

Maybe the prevalence of malice-free dipsh*ttery isn't such a perplexity when you consider the level of intelligence displayed by people today, especially in America. The Butterball turkey company offers a hotline that customers can call for advice on roasting their bird. They post online some of the dumbest questions people ask. Here are a few examples:

"I carved my turkey with a chain saw. Is the chain grease going to adversely affect my turkey?"

"How do I roast my turkey so it gets golden brown tan lines in the shape of a turkey bikini?"

"Can I thaw my turkey in the toilet?"

"My cat started eating my raw turkey. What do I do?"

"How can I thaw my turkey on my car luggage rack [while driving]?"

"My turkey thawed on my lap. Can I eat it?"

The burning question before us may not be how dipsh*ttery can occur without malice. The real issue may be why we haven't been destroyed by it, considering the people we have to deal with.

* * *

"Stupidity is the same as evil if you judge by the results."
– Margaret Atwood

Chapter Nine

The Eighth Law: As Dipsh*ts Increase Numerically, Dipsh*ttery Increases Exponentially

If you search Google News for stories of people who waged a standoff with police after barricading themselves inside, you may be surprised to discover how frequently it happens. As usual, the United States leads the world. The following cases happened during a single week.

Jersey Joy Ride. Malik Moore, a 45-year-old New Jersey man, might end up on Santa's "naughty" list this year. Police in the town of Guttenberg said that Moore stole a car and crashed it a short time later, injuring a pedestrian in the process. Then he got out and assaulted a bystander, they said. Next, Moore reportedly broke into a residence and assaulted one of its residents. The occupants managed to escape as Moore barricaded himself inside.

Police responded and surrounded the home. A seven-hour standoff ensued, during which neighbors were removed from the area by police. Moore was finally arrested by a tactical response team. It's unclear from news reports whether he surrendered or was taken by force. The condition of Malik's victims has not been disclosed.

Skillet Scofflaw. Police in a Los Angeles suburb responded to a call about an armed assault at a residence. Upon arriving at the address, they found a 50-year-old man with a contusion and a 45-year-old female with a stab wound. The woman told police that an assailant had conked the man with a cast iron skillet.

The suspect, whose name has not been released, barricaded himself inside the house and held cops at bay for five hours. Neighbors had to evacuate during the ordeal. Finally, police made the call to deploy tear gas. A SWAT team then was able to take the offender into custody.

Florida Fusillade. An unnamed man and woman drove to an apartment to visit a relative in Lakeland, a city 56 miles west of Orlando. Upon arriving the man, age 35, spoke with his relative in the parking lot while the woman waited in the car. It's not clear from news reports whether Miguel Angel Ruiz Borges is the relative or whether he's a third party who joined the conversation. But at some point, Borges pulled a gun and shot the man in the heat of an argument. The victim was rushed to the emergency room and is expected to recover.

Police soon arrived and found that Borges had barricaded himself inside an apartment. The terrified woman who lived there locked herself and her three-year-old child in a bedroom. Police quickly helped them escape through a window. Meanwhile, Borges stalled the police for two hours before surrendering.

Country Roads, Take Me Home. A West Virginia woman called police to report that a man she had a protective order against was following her on the highway. Officers tried to get Nathan Cunningham, age 20, to pull over, but he led them on a high-speed chase. Cunningham made it home and barricaded himself inside. Only after relatives appealed to him to come out did the suspect surrender.

According to WOWK-TV, Cunningham "is charged with violating a protective order that followed another incident where he was later charged for strangulation. Police say they saw a message where he said he was going to shoot police and told the victim he was going to kill her and her family." West Virginia State University went into lockdown until this heinous hillbilly was arrested.

Hunting Drones Out of Season. Jonathan L. Harville, age 57, of Elizabethtown, Kentucky, faces a host of charges, including attempted murder, that could land him in prison for decades. It all began when Harville's wife reported that she was hiding from her husband in their basement, because he was brandishing a rifle. When sheriff's deputies arrived, Harville reportedly opened fire. He also fired at a passing motorist, police said. Harville then barricaded himself inside and held off the cops for nearly four hours, firing several shots during the standoff, according to the report.

Police deployed a drone to surveille the situation, and Harville allegedly shot it down. His wife remained trapped in the basement throughout the ordeal. When negotiations failed, a SWAT team deployed tear gas and stormed the home to nab this Kentucky commando.

During the week when the above incidents occurred, I found reports of at least 20 such incidents in the United States alone. Just imagine the year-in and year-out impact of barricaded dipsh*ts on communities worldwide. Their rash and futile attempts to avoid arrest draw an overwhelming police response, terrify and sometimes harm hostages, displace neighbors, and unnerve neighborhoods. That doesn't even take into account property damage. They vividly exemplify the eighth law: "As dipsh*ts increase numerically, dipsh*ttery increases exponentially."

The above cases are so similar in their toxic effects that I'll only prepare a dipsh*t analysis for the worst of them, which undoubtedly is Malik Moore. According to news reports, he stole and totaled a car, injured a pedestrian, assaulted two more people, broke into a home, barricaded himself inside, caused the evacuation of neighbors, and held off police for several hours. Here's my assessment of Moore's dipsh*ttery:

- **Behavior:** chronic
- **Situation:** benign (We don't know what set off his crime spree. Was he high on something or perhaps undergoing a psychotic episode? If I knew him to be profoundly mentally ill, I wouldn't apply the dipsh*t label. But neither drug-induced intoxication nor manageable psychological issues can justify his behavior. Nothing about the external situation forced him to run amok.)
- **Cause:** habitual (Judging by the events of this day, I suspect this kind of behavior is par for the course.)
- **Outcome:** 5 (destructive) for Moore; 4 or 5 (damaging or destructive) for the pedestrian he hit, depending on seriousness of his or her injuries; 4 (damaging) for the two people he assaulted and also for the people who had to flee their home when Moore broke in; 3 (disruptive) for neighbors who had to be evacuated during the standoff; 2 (imposing) for the police, prosecutor, and court.

Now that these holed-up hooligans have demonstrated the exponential destructiveness of dipsh*ts in small numbers, let's look at some other types of cases. Remember Kenny Wells, who tried to sneak a gun through an airport security checkpoint during holiday travel season? He caused a stampede of passengers, an airport lockdown, flight interruptions, missed connections, and countless re-bookings. His noxious and selfish act rippled from airport to airport. If one obtuse, offensive pest can wreak so much havoc, consider the tsunami of destruction that would await us if chronic types ever got organized and acted in unison. Fortunately for us, "getting their act together" is not one of their strong points.

Baby on Board. Adalyn Burkett, age 18, was babysitting two toddlers in Florida when she and her boyfriend, Marquan Edwards, 22, allegedly abducted the tots and fled the state in a stolen truck. Burkett was supposed to watch the children overnight and return them the next morning. She also had permission to use the mother's pickup truck during that time. When the mom discovered her kids and the truck missing that next day, she notified police. Thus began a multi-state manhunt for the kidnappers and the children.

Burkett and Edwards headed for Milwaukee, Wisconsin, over 1,000 miles from the toddlers' home in the Florida panhandle. Both abductors have ties to that city, police said. At some point, the pair became aware of the frantic search for the children and decided to abandon them. They left the two toddlers alone in a public park. Thankfully, the children were recovered by police, apparently uninjured. Burkett and Edwards were apprehended in

Milwaukee, and the kids were reunited with family members. The kidnappers' motives have not been revealed.

Dipsh*t analytics for the babysitter from hell and her beau:

- **Behavior:** chronic
- **Situation:** benign (How does a babysitting gig lead to car theft and interstate flight?)
- **Cause:** self-induced (At minimum this was self-induced, but they could be habitual types.)
- **Outcome:** 5 (destructive) for Burkett and Edwards as well as the children's mother and extended family members; 3 (disruptive) for the toddlers, who are too young to retain long-term memories of the kidnapping, but may have been terrified by the incomprehensible events; 3 (disruptive) for police in multiple states who were part of the search; 2 (imposing) for Milwaukee cops who apprehended the pair and also for the criminal justice system.

Putting the "Pee" in impure. Thirteen women working in a Houston office building filed a lawsuit against several companies who they say allowed a janitor to remain on the job after he was caught on video peeing into the employees' water bottles. One of the victims reportedly turned the video over to the property managers. She said they assured her something would be done and asked her to not tell other employees until they had a chance to respond. She complied, and the janitor, Lucio Catarino Diaz, age 50, was allowed to continue working for several more days.

Diaz admitted to dribbling in the water bottles, KRIV-TV reported. But that's just the good news. Here's the bad news: All thirteen women tested positive for Herpes Simplex 1 Virus, according to their lawsuit, a condition that also reportedly afflicts Diaz. The wee-weeing janitor was charged with "assault with a deadly weapon." (Yes, really.)

Dipsh*t analytics for Diaz, the janitor known for giving of himself:

- **Behavior:** chronic
- **Situation:** benign
- **Cause:** self-induced (He could be a habitual type, but he was holding a job at the time, and we have no knowledge of other possible malfeasance.)
- **Outcome:** 5 (destructive) for the thirteen victims and their families as well as for Diaz and his family, if he has one; 4 (damaging) for other employees who fear that they were exposed to Diaz's urine but who have not tested positive for Herpes; 4 (damaging) for the companies being sued; 2 (imposing) for the police, prosecutor, and court.

Ill Will. A federal judge sentenced Amanda Christine Riley, age 36, to five years in prison for fraud in connection with her solicitation of donations for cancer treatments – a disease she never had. Riley, a San Jose, California resident, began claiming in 2012 that she'd been diagnosed with Hodgkin's lymphoma. She cultivated social media followers whom she duped with tales of her fictitious struggle to survive the phantom disease. She even shaved her head to further the scam.

The Justice Department said in a news release that Riley "falsified medical records...forged physicians' letters and medical certifications...convinced family members to echo her false claims...gave materially false testimony in several legal proceedings...[and] attacked anyone who suggested she was malingering (going so far as to sue one of them)." She got away with the scam for six years and raised $105,513 from 349 victims until the Internal Revenue Service exposed her deception, authorities said.

In 2000 Marc D. Feldman, M.D. introduced the term, *Munchausen by Internet*, to indicate Riley's type of malingering – faking illness online for fun and profit. *Munchausen syndrome* (now known as *factitious disorder*) refers to someone who either fakes or induces illness or injury to him- or herself for attention and sympathy. When someone, typically a parent or caregiver, causes illness or injury to a dependent person for the same sympathy and attention, it's called *Munchausen by proxy* (or *factitious disorder imposed on another*).

Feldman was the first medical professional to document the phenomenon of factitious individuals extending this scam from the real world to the Internet. Social media in particular has given malingerers a much wider reach and a far greater pool of potential victims. Riley's con game is remarkable for its longevity, its financial success, and the elaborate deception that enabled it.

Dipsh*t analytics for Amanda Christine "Finally Cancer Free!" Riley:

- **Behavior:** chronic

- **Situation:** benign (This is a tough call, because we don't know if there was a financial crisis that motivated this behavior. If there was, the situation could have been frenetic or even provocative. But typically, Munchausen is more about attention-seeking. So I'm going with benign.)
- **Cause:** self-induced (I wouldn't disagree if someone argued that she was a habitual type. We're not sure either way.)
- **Outcome:** 5 (destructive) for Riley and her family; 3 (disruptive) for her donors who learned they'd been suckered; (2) imposing for the investigators, prosecutor, and court.

Souls Adrift

It's no exaggeration to say that the pandemic knocked the world off its axis, metaphorically speaking. Isolation, sickness and death, loss of jobs, shuttering of businesses, disruption of children's education, and political turmoil regarding masks and vaccines are just a few of the tectonic shifts that unmoored billions of people from normality. It's understandable and yet dismaying how much COVID-19 has changed us.

Emile Durkheim (1858 – 1917), a French philosopher and pioneer in the field of sociology, sought to understand the feelings of anguish, hopelessness, and futility that drive people to suicide. In his seminal book, *On Suicide*, Durkheim wrote, "When life is not worth living, everything becomes a pretext for ridding ourselves of it." He observed a connection between this death wish and social turmoil, noting that "there is a collective mood, as there is an individual mood, [and] individuals are too closely involved in the life of society for it to be sick without their being affected. Its suffering inevitably becomes theirs."

Anomie theory is Durkheim's explanation of how and why people become alienated from society during periods of rapid social change. ("Anomie" means absence of accepted social norms.) When masses of individuals experience a disconnect between their aspirations and the means available to achieve them, there is a corresponding rise in deviant or destructive behavior. Obviously, social problems and political strife existed before COVID-19, but the disease caused disruptions that accelerated anomie.

Following in Durkheim's footsteps, sociologist Robert K. Merton (often credited as the founder of modern sociology) introduced *strain theory*. When limited opportunities and structural barriers prevent people from achieving financial success, social status, or similar goals, they experience strain or frustration. This creates an incentive for individuals to use deviant methods in pursuit of their ambitions. For example, people from marginalized or disadvantaged backgrounds may engage in criminal activities when access to legitimate opportunities is denied them.

In 2015 economists Anne Case and Angus Deaton coined the term, *diseases of despair*. They observed that death rates among middle-aged white Americans were increasing, even as mortality for other demographic groups was in decline. Their investigation of this anomaly revealed three main causes – suicide, drug overdoses, and alcohol-induced liver disease (i.e., despair-based factors). A report by the Penn State College of Medicine identified "financial instability, lack of infrastructure, a deteriorating sense of community and family fragmentation...[as] key contributors to diseases of despair." The opioid epidemic is an example of the devastation that our societal dysfunction has spawned.

When we look beyond middle-aged whites and at society generally, other diseases of despair become apparent. Mass shootings have increased in post-pandemic America, as have carjackings, homelessness, and petty crime in our cities. A cursory review of news headlines suggests that other Western nations are experiencing similar side effects of COVID-19 (minus the gunfire). These problems existed before but are worse now. As anomie spreads and strain affects more and more people, these problems will increase, absent comprehensive, effective programs to restore civility to society. Given the current political climate, the prospects for restorative action are not promising.

Social exclusion theory is the result of research by several scholars in psychology, sociology, and economics. It explains how unequal power, limited resources, and lack of opportunities block people from social, economic, and political participation, whether intentionally or not. When these barriers persist as entrenched facts of life, both individuals and society itself suffer the consequences. Exclusion can extend to economic, educational, political, health, cultural, and technological aspects of life. For example, many rural areas in America lack access to reliable broadband Internet. And even in urban areas, many households cannot afford it.

Quite a few of the social phenomena presented in these chapters – Karens, disruptive airline passengers, and barricaded bullies, for example – can be better understood in light of anomie, social strain, social exclusion, and diseases of despair. The importance of acceptance, belonging, and knowing that one is a valued and useful member of society cannot be understated. Nihilistic disconnectedness is a breeding ground for dipsh*ttery, and we all suffer the consequences.

Fyre > Ready > Aim

Dipsh*ts need not be individuals acting alone. If one noxious pest can unleash exponential destruction, just imagine how devastating a team of them can be. The Fyre Festival is such a case. It represents a trifecta of incompetence, irresponsibility, and criminality.

The Fyre Festival was a heavily promoted, luxury music festival scheduled to take place in the Bahamas in April 2017. Conceived by entrepreneur Billy McFarland and rapper Ja Rule, the event was promoted on social media as an exclusive experience featuring famous musicians, gourmet food, and luxurious accommodations.

Tickets for the festival ranged from $500 to $1,500 for general admission. VIP packages costing up to $12,000 offered meet-and-greet opportunities with the artists, premium accommodations, and other upgrades. Private villas, yacht charters, and customized experiences could be arranged for prices as high as $250,000.

When the event date arrived, festival-goers arrived at the venue to encounter what can be bluntly (but accurately) described as a sh*tshow. Instead of the luxurious villas and deluxe accommodations that were advertised, attendees found half-built tents lacking proper bedding. Many of these were soggy from recent rain. There was a shortage of clean water, so attendees resorted to drinking whatever bottled water they could scrounge. Rather than gourmet meals, cheese sandwiches were on the menu. Few arrangements had been made for medical care and security.

Logistical failures and lack of coordination left some attendees stranded on the island with no means of returning to the mainland. Flights were canceled or delayed, leaving many ticketholders frightened and desperate. Chaotic scenes and substandard conditions were documented by the victims and shared on social media. Images of squalor, unappetizing food, and frantic music fans quickly went viral, drawing widespread disbelief and outrage.

In the aftermath of this debacle, McFarland was convicted of multiple counts of fraud. He deceived both investors and attendees by falsely representing the festival's infrastructure, amenities, and overall feasibility. McFarland and his team lied about the event's capabilities in order to generate hype and boost ticket sales. McFarland's deceit was a key factor in the festival's failure. Ja Rule faced some lawsuits afterwards but was not implicated in the fraudulent activities. He faced no criminal charges. In the final analysis, the Fyre Festival never stood a chance because of bogus claims, financial malfeasance, and inept logistics.

There are many parallels between the collapse of FTX, a cryptocurrency exchange, and the Fyre Festival's failure to launch. Both were the handiwork of young entrepreneurs who proved to be "not ready for prime time." Sam Bankman-Fried, FTX's CEO and founder, allegedly used clients' money to bail out his other company, Alameda Research. The Justice Department and the Securities and Exchange Commission are investigating this as well as allegations that the company made false and misleading statements to investors. Suspicions of fraud and financial mismanagement abound. Sound familiar?

Sam Bankman-Fried has been extradited to the United States from the Bahamas and awaits trial. FTX filed for bankruptcy in November 2022 after a bailout attempt by Binance, a rival crypto exchange, failed. The number of investors who lost money is unknown, but estimates range as high as one million people. Financial losses are still being tallied but could be in the billions. One investor told the BBC that he lost $110,000 in the collapse. Bankruptcy filings show that FTX had $3.1 billion in assets when it failed and about $8 billion in liabilities.

No discussion of young entrepreneurs who flamed-out spectacularly would be complete without including Elizabeth Holmes and her erstwhile blood-testing startup, Theranos. Holmes now sits in federal prison. That's quite a come-down for someone who hobnobbed with Bill Clinton and duped the likes of Henry Kissinger and William Perry, former Secretaries of State, and Jim Mattis, former four-star general, all members of her board.

Theranos began with Holmes' vision of developing blood-testing technology that could diagnose multiple medical problems from a single drop of blood. When the company was unable to engineer devices capable of doing this, Holmes and her team resorted to deception as well as legal threats when insiders raised concerns.

The company's Edison machines frequently malfunctioned. Theranos's testing lab produced unreliable test results, thereby placing patients' health in jeopardy. In some cases, Theranos was found to be testing expired blood, and federal inspectors determined that the lab had neither the equipment nor proper staffing to maintain quality control. Even though Theranos knew of these deficiencies, regulators and patients were never notified that test results might be inaccurate.

A *Wall Street Journal* exposé that revealed the company's failures and duplicity set off a death spiral of revelations and defections that ultimately destroyed the company. Holmes and Theranos's president, Ramesh "Sunny" Balwani, were convicted of multiple counts of wire fraud. Holmes drew a sentence of 11 years and 3 months while Balsani got 12 years and 11 months.

The dipsh*t analytics for McFarland, Bankman-Fried, and Holmes would be so similar that I'm only preparing one composite assessment for the three of them. Here's how I view the catastrophic effects of their malfeasance:

- **Behavior:** chronic.
- **Situation:** frenetic
- **Cause:** habitual (These companies essentially took on the Machiavellian personalities of their founders.)
- **Outcome:** 5 (destructive) for the terrible threesome, their families, and people in their immediate orbit, such as major investors and board members; 4 (damaging) for employees and for customers, festival-goers, patients, vendors, creditors, etc.; 2 (imposing) for investigators, prosecutors, and courts.

Foibles, Fantasies, and Folly

The Fyre Festival, FTX, and Theranos all began with an entrepreneurial vision. To paraphrase the bard, that's the stuff dreams are made of. But when dreams can't be brought to fruition, they're just fantasies. If an entrepreneur has to resort to fraud to execute his or her vision, then either the business idea is not well-conceived or that individual is not competent for the task at hand.

Assume for the moment that McFarland, Bankman-Fried, and Holmes all began with the best of intentions and wanted to operate legitimately profitable businesses. What are some possible explanations for their extreme deviation from the straight and narrow? The following theories may provide some answers.

In 1993 business professors Dean C. Ludwig and Clinton O. Longnecker published "The Bathsheba Syndrome: The Ethical Failure of Successful Leaders." The authors noted that egregious ethical or criminal behavior by corporate executives is frequently attributed to external factors, such as highly competitive market conditions. "Competitive pressures," it was assumed, incentivized leaders to do bad things. And sometimes that's true. Ludwig and Longnecker observed, however, that misconduct is often the by-product of success itself. They called this phenomenon the *Bathsheba syndrome.*

The Bible tells the story of King David's lust for Bathsheba, a beautiful Israelite. One night he saw her taking a bath on her rooftop, and David (being the horndog that he was) wanted her. Bathsheba was the wife of Uriah, one of David's soldiers, who was away fighting for king and country.

David invited Bathsheba to his quarters and there engaged in horizontal refreshment with her. Some time later, she turned up pregnant. Virgin births were not introduced until the New Testament, so David faced exposure as an adulterer. To remedy this problem, he summoned Uriah from the battlefield on the assumption that he would sleep with Bathsheba. But Uriah slept alone. This forced King Horndog to come up with "Plan B."

David summoned Joab, Uriah's commander, and ordered him to put Uriah on the front line. Then, in the heat of battle, Joab was to withdraw his men, leaving Uriah exposed. Enemy troops would hastily dispatch Bathsheba's husband, and the widow would become available. David would then be able to consort with her without committing adultery. He could even acknowledge his contribution to her pregnancy. (The plan worked. Don't you just love a happy ending?)

An intoxicating combination of lust and absolute power corrupted David. He believed he could fornicate, impregnate, and assassinate with impunity. The Bathsheba syndrome denotes malignant leadership behavior when it is caused by internal flaws rather than external exigencies. Becoming power-mad, feeling entitled and unaccountable, or putting personal ambition above the organization's best interests are familiar examples.

McFarland, Bankman-Fried, and Holmes were prime candidates for succumbing to the dark side of success. All were young visionaries operating speculative, high-profile, big-money businesses. McFarland and Holmes are college dropouts. Bankman-Fried graduated from Massachusetts Institute of Technology, but like the other two he seems to have gotten "too big for his britches," as we Southerners say. Like Icarus, these upstarts flew too high and were brought down by their own heedlessness.

Of course, there are other possible explanations for why McFarland, Bankman-Friend, and Holmes failed so spectacularly:

- *Financial incentives theory* suggests that leaders may engage in questionable behavior when their compensation is closely tied to financial performance metrics. If their bonuses, stock options, or other incentives are based on meeting specific targets, leaders may feel compelled to manipulate financial data to achieve those goals, even if it involves unethical or fraudulent practices.

- When there are *inadequate internal controls* and oversight procedures within an organization, leaders may find it easier to engage in malfeasance without getting caught. They may conclude that there's a low risk of detection and punishment.

- Executives, especially those in publicly traded companies, face pressure from investors and financial markets to deliver short-term results. *Short-termism and pressure from investors* can create a culture focused on immediate financial gains without regard to the methods used to achieve them.

- In some cases, corporate leaders may engage in fraudulent behavior because of *groupthink*, a psychological phenomenon whereby people value consensus and harmony over debate, disagreement, critical thinking and ethical decision-making. If a leadership team becomes insular and conformist in their thinking, they may turn a blind eye to malfeasance.

- *Personal financial pressures or a personal crisis* can tempt leaders to commit fraud. Mounting debts or family obligations can drive individuals to take risks that they would be reluctant to entertain under less stressful conditions.
- *Organizational Culture* plays a significant role in shaping workplace behavior. Wherever unethical practices are tolerated or even encouraged, leaders can become emboldened to lie, cheat, or commit fraud.

Each case is different, of course, and it's likely that a combination of factors, both internal and external, contributed to each of these spectacular flame-outs. None of that changes the fact that the actions of these three were ultimately stupid and despicable. They're crème de la dipsh*ts.

Brandolini's Law

Alberto Brandolini, an Italian software engineer, is credited with originating the "law" that bears his name: "The amount of energy needed to refute bullsh*t is an order of magnitude bigger than to produce it." An "order of magnitude" is roughly ten times the original amount. Brandolini is essentially saying that the BS generated by one dipsh*t creates exponential ripple effects that require ten times the amount of effort to refute. His law aligns quite well with the eighth law of dipsh*ttery.

As an example, consider that in April and June of 2020, "Facebook removed more than seven million pieces of harmful COVID-19 misinformation, including claims relating to false cures or suggestions that social distancing is ineffective," according to Yahoo! News. Or recall how Donald Trump's claims that "the election was rigged" precipitated an insurrection. His diehard fans continue to believe that. Another politician, Robert F. Kennedy, Jr. is now spreading the claim that vaccines cause autism.

In *The Life-Changing Science of Detecting Bullsh*t*, psychologist John V. Petrocelli makes an important distinction between BS and lies. A liar knows he or she is lying and intends to deceive. A bullsh*tter may believe the BS or may not care whether it's true or not. But both liars and bullsh*tters put the burden on others to apply critical thinking, seek out evidence pro or con, and refute the falsehoods.

When I was a child, it was common for parents to urge children to clean their plates by saying, "Children are starving in China." There's a shocking story behind that childhood admonition. In 1958, China's supreme leader, Mao Zedong, declared a national war on agricultural pests. He decided that rats, flies, mosquitoes, and sparrows were consuming or damaging stored grain, thereby creating shortages. The entire nation was ordered to prioritize eliminating these threats.

The eradication of sparrows was so successful that populations of locusts and other crop-destroying insects exploded. With their avian predators decimated, the bugs proliferated out of control. Within two years, the plan had to be abandoned. In 1962, China had to import 250,000 sparrows from the Soviet Union to fight the pestilence of insects.

Mao's unsubstantiated assumption that sparrows were causing grain shortages resulted in a famine that killed about 36 million people—*six times more than died in the Holocaust.* The tragedy was exacerbated by the fact that no one was prepared to tell Chairman

Mao that he was wrong. (And yes, I'm calling him Comrade Dipsh*t).

As we've seen, whether the perpetrator is a criminal lowlife barricaded inside a home, a massively bankrolled entrepreneur, or a national leader, when he or she behaves incompetently and irresponsibly, the consequences can reverberate exponentially.

* * *

"The totally convinced and the totally stupid have too much in common for the resemblance to be accidental."
– Robert Anton Wilson

Chapter Ten

The Ninth Law: Any Well-meaning Attempt to Intervene with a Dipsh*t is Likely to Result in the Intervention Itself Descending into Dipsh*ttery (See Third Law)

The term, "good Samaritan," as you probably know, comes from the biblical parable of a traveler from Samaria who stopped to help a Jew who had been badly beaten. The victim had been robbed and bludgeoned nearly to death. Two pious Jews had passed by and rendered no aid. But the Samaritan took pity on the dying man. He treated the man's wounds, took him to an inn, and paid for all expenses until the victim recovered. (The Jews and Samaritans were traditional enemies over religious and ethnic differences.)

In researching cases for this book of people acting as good Samaritans, I was surprised to discover how frequently these well-meaning individuals end up as victims because of their intervention. News stories alternate between reports of altruistic people who valiantly aid or rescue someone in distress, and would-be rescuers who themselves become victims when they attempt to render assistance.

We're predisposed to help each other, whether as a show of support or in times of need. People contribute to GoFundMe appeals from total strangers when the need is real and urgent. Many bloggers and influencers rely on Patreon contributions from appreciative fans. Whenever people lose their homes and possessions to a hurricane, wildfire, or tornado, an outpouring of generosity is sure to follow.

This tendency of human beings to display benevolence and generosity in times of crisis is a welcome counterpoint to the endless torrent of dipsh*ttery in the world. Kindness is an underrated virtue, and it's frequently in short supply. But there must be a balance between goodwill and prudence. Otherwise, we leave ourselves vulnerable to unnecessary risks. It's one thing to donate funds to help a community devastated by a flood, but it's quite another to make a habit of picking up hitchhikers.

The ninth law warns that trying to assist or rescue a dipsh*t will probably result in your being swallowed up, metaphorically speaking, in a vortex of ignorance, incompetence, and irresponsibility. Come within the gravitational pull of Planet Dipsh*t, and you'll probably wish you hadn't. The following cases feature some good Samaritans who found that out the hard way.

Shake, Rattle, and Roll. A man driving on I-94 in St. Paul, Minnesota, observed a vehicle crash and roll over. He stopped to help. Two survivors, a man and woman, emerged from the wreck (it's unclear which of them was driving). The male crash victim ran from the scene. The woman, later identified as Sydney Ann McKellepp, age 22, allegedly shoved the good Samaritan out of the way and commandeered his vehicle. He tried to stop her, but she dragged him a short distance before speeding away, police said. Officers reportedly arrived just in time to witness the scuffle.

According to the arrest report, McKellepp fled from police, leading them on a high-speed chase that ended only when they forcibly disabled the stolen vehicle. They first blew her tires with spike strips, but she continued fleeing. Finally, an officer rammed her and terminated the chase. McKellepp had outstanding warrants and a revoked driver's license, police said. Oh, and McKellepp's vehicle that rolled over on I-94 – it too reportedly was stolen. She has refused to identify the male passenger who fled.

Dipsh*t analytics for this alleged maven of mayhem:

- **Behavior:** chronic
- **Situation:** provocative (We don't know what caused the rollover or what transpired leading up to it. But the vehicle apparently was stolen and McKellepp had outstanding warrants. So at the time she encountered the good Samaritan, her situation was provocative – she faced imminent arrest.)
- **Cause:** habitual (Yes, she was triggered by panic after the rollover, and her alleged criminal past likely included many self-induced choices. But in view of this episode and the outstanding warrants against her, I see her behavior as persistent and habitual.)
- **Outcome:** 5 (destructive) for McKellepp; 4 (damaging) for the good Samaritan; 3, 4, or 5 (disruptive, damaging, or destructive) for the male occupant of the rollover vehicle, depending on whether he is caught and what consequences, if any, he suffers; 3 (disruptive) for officers who

had to engage in a high-speed chase and ram McKellepp's vehicle; 2 (imposing) for the prosecutor and court.

Bleak Midwinter. A Colorado woman stopped her car in Denver to help a homeless man. She let him get inside to warm up from the frigid March winds. After he got out, she noticed her cell phone was missing. She then approached a group of homeless people to see if they knew the man. They did know him and agreed to help her track him down.

Back in the car, the homeless helpers directed the woman to a certain area when they believed the man could be found. Upon arrival, she got out to look for him, leaving her 2020 Alfa-Romeo running with her dog and the homeless people inside. (See where this is going?)

No sooner had this do-gooder turned her back than her passengers absconded with the car and her dog. She filed a police report, and understandably was concerned mostly about her dog. But no information is available as to whether she got her phone, her car, or her dog back.

A good Samaritan as caring, trusting, and kind-hearted as this woman didn't deserve to be treated with such cruelty. No one does. But her experience illustrates the risk of intervening with dipsh*ts. In hindsight, she should have chalked up the theft of her phone as a lesson learned: Do not get involved with homeless people except in a controlled environment, such as a soup kitchen or shelter, or perhaps when accompanied by others you know and trust. Being homeless shouldn't brand someone as a villain. But some people who are dangerous or criminally inclined end up homeless – and desperate circumstances can only make bad people more inclined to victimize others.

The dipsh*ts in this case are the stupid and despicable people who took advantage of her naivety and generosity. This good Samaritan may have been unwise during these encounters, but I wouldn't call her stupid. And she certainly wasn't despicable – quite the opposite.

Dipsh*t analytics for these people with no home and no heart:

- **Behavior:** chronic
- **Situation:** frenetic (I'm sure circumstances are usually frenetic, and often provocative, for people living on the streets.)
- **Cause:** habitual (These were opportunistic crimes and self-induced, but I'm betting that this kind of behavior is the norm for desperate people with nothing to lose.)
- **Outcome:** 5 (destructive) for the good Samaritan, which I base on my own reaction if someone stole my beloved pet and I feared for its safety; a rating of 0 to 4 for the homeless people, depending on whether they escape punishment or suffer some kind of legal retribution; 2 (imposing) for the police and possibly for the prosecutor and court if anyone is arrested and charged.

Mick the Knife. On the outskirts of Belfast, Northern Ireland, a motorist came upon a body lying in the road. Assuming that the man had been injured, the driver got out to render aid.

A second man then emerged from the bushes and jumped in the car. He failed to steal it, because the good Samaritan had pocketed his keys. But the man in the road got up and attacked the traveler, slashing him with a knife. The assailant got away with £750 and a cell phone. The victim's family offered a reward and appealed for video evidence.

Terminated Texas-Style. One night in Houston, three men entered a smoke stop and held up the clerk at gunpoint. As they exited the store, a witness in the parking lot pulled his pistol and ordered the robbers to stop. A gunfight ensued during which the would-be good Samaritan was shot and killed. None of the bandits appeared to have been wounded, police said. The three will be charged with aggravated robbery and murder when apprehended.

Roadside Distraction. A man driving in Franklin, Tennessee noticed a truck by the roadside that appeared to have broken down. Two men in their twenties were standing near it. The motorist stopped to see if the men needed help, and they replied that their truck needed a jump start. When the motorist got out of his vehicle, one of the men jumped in and stole it. The other man drove off in the supposedly disabled truck. Composite sketches of the carjackers were circulated in hopes of identifying them.

The previous three cases are alike in that the suspects remain unknown, and the facts are straightforward – a good Samaritan intervened and immediately suffered the consequences. Here is a composite analysis for the villains in all three cases:

- **Behavior:** chronic

- **Situation:** benign, except for the store robbery, which was provocative
- **Cause:** habitual (All three cases involve premeditated, violent crimes, which I think implies more than just a self-induced episode.)
- **Outcome:** 0 or 5 (null or destructive) for the criminals, depending on whether they are caught and punished, or whether they evade arrest; 5 for the good Samaritan who died and 4 for those who were robbed; 0 or 2 (null or imposing) for the police, prosecutors, and courts depending on whether the crooks are arrested and tried.

Victimized do-gooders perfectly illustrate the principle that intervening with obtuse and offensive people is fraught with risk. Good Samaritans serve as vivid examples because they are well-meaning and motivated by goodwill. They can't know in advance whether the person they're helping is toxic. But not all interventions involve strangers helping strangers. In some cases, a relative, friend, neighbor, or co-worker intercedes with a person they know – someone they should realize is Trouble with a capital "T." Let's look at some of those cases.

The Big Sleep. One night in Conroe, Texas, 38-year-old Francisco Oropeza thought it would be a good idea to go out into his front yard and start firing his AR-15 semi-automatic rifle. His neighbor, Wilson Garcia, approached their adjoining fence and asked Oropeza to stop shooting. It was about 11:00 p.m., and Garcia informed his neighbor that his baby was trying to sleep.

Oropeza, who was reportedly drunk, retorted that he'd do anything he damned pleased in his own yard. According to police,

Oropeza is a Mexican national who has been deported several times from the U.S. Garcia and his family are from Honduras. News reports indicate that these neighbors were once on friendly terms but relations between them may have turned sour.

Shortly after Garcia asked him to stop shooting, Oropeza barged into Garcia's house and killed five people, including a child. The victims, male and female, ranged in age from 8 to 25. Garcia himself was wounded but survived.

A manhunt for the shooter soon commenced as Oropeza went into hiding. Police caught up with him a few days later and charged him with the murders. He was preparing to flee to Mexico, police said.

Dipsh*t analytics for the neighbor from hell:

- **Behavior:** chronic
- **Situation:** provocative
- **Cause:** habitual (For behavior this extreme, I'm assuming the worst. It's unlikely this was a rare, self-induced episode of misconduct.)
- **Outcome:** 5 (destructive) for Oropeza, Garcia, and the victims; 3 (disruptive) for that neighborhood and the town of Conroe; 2 (imposing) for the police, prosecutor, and court.

Door Jam. Susan Lorincz, age 58, of Marion County, Florida, called the sheriff's department many times to complain about neighborhood children. "The kids keep running back and forth over here," she said during one call. Another time, she complained of "the children screaming their fool heads off, running around."

During their response to one of Lorincz's calls, one deputy was heard saying, "Did we explain to her there doesn't need to be a call for service every time the kids are playing in the road or in the yard?"

Lorincz, who is white, had a history of shouting at the children of Ajike "AJ" Owens, who is black and lived across the street. During one encounter, Lorincz reportedly threw a roller skate at one of the kids and broke his "tablet" (presumably an iPad or similar device). When Owens found out about this, she went to Lorincz's home and knocked on her door. The 35-year-old mother reportedly was fed up with Lorincz's vicious treatment of her children. Lorincz responded to Owens' knocking by shooting and killing her through the closed door.

Today this gunslinging granny faces trial for manslaughter. Relatives say that the children are grieving for the sudden and violent death of their mother and suffering profound guilt for being the reason their mother confronted her killer. This tragic episode culminated a feud between these neighbors that spanned over two years.

Dipsh*t analytics for Susan "Doorbuster" Lorincz:

- **Behavior:** chronic
- **Situation:** frenetic (Children playing loudly near an older person's home could be disturbing. But that's life, not an excuse for police reports or aggression toward children.)
- **Cause:** triggered (She was clearly afraid of dealing with the children's angry mother – but she brought that on herself.)
- **Outcome:** 5 (destructive) for Lorincz, Owens, the children, and extended family members; 3 (disruptive) for the

neighborhood; 2 (imposing) for the police, prosecutor, and court.

Sun and Gun. On the fourth of July 2023 a group enjoying the beach in Tampa, Florida was alarmed to see people riding jet skis near children in shallow water. They called out to the jet skiers, warning them of the danger they were creating. This provoked an argument, and both groups began shooting at each other. Hearing shots fired, an elderly man hustled his 7-year-old grandson into his truck, and they both laid down. Unfortunately, this protective maneuver failed. A bullet penetrated the truck, entered the boy's brain, and killed him. The grandfather was also wounded but survived. Police are searching for the suspects.

A couple of important lessons can be learned from this case. First, the people who challenged the jet skiers were right. Not only were they correct to perceive the danger, but they also acted responsibly by warning the jet skiers to move away from the children. The ninth law advises that interacting with dipsh*ts usually ramps up the dipsh*ttery. That's certainly true in this case – but it was necessary for the people on shore to get involved anyway. Second, the consequences of interacting with dipsh*ts may fall harder on innocent bystanders than on those who intervene. There's no report of anyone being injured from this exchange of gunfire except for the boy and his grandfather.

Dipsh*t analytics for these sinister stormers of the beach:

- **Behavior:** chronic
- **Situation:** benign (Only their misconduct made it provocative.)

- **Cause:** self-induced (Possibly habitual, but we don't know.)
- **Outcome:** 5 (destructive) for the boy, his grandfather, and their families; 4 (damaging) for the people on the beach who probably only fired in self-defense (no indication that they were arrested); 0 or 5 (null or destructive) for the jet skiers, depending on whether they are caught and punished or manage to elude capture; 2 (imposing) for the police, prosecutor, and court.

A Farewell to Harms. Drew McKeown, age 37, an ex-soldier, faces ten years in prison for rape and theft. He showed up at an elderly woman's flat in Blaenau Gwent, Wales, and she invited him in. It's unclear how they knew each other or why he came to her door that day.

The victim, whose identity is protected by the court, testified that she caught McKeown stealing her cigarettes. Taking pity on him, she gave them to him and bought him a train ticket so he could travel to Newcastle. He repaid her kindness by sexually assaulting her repeatedly.

After the assaults, McKeown refused to leave her flat and demanded that she make coffee for him. He stayed the night and slept in the bed with her. The next morning, he departed to catch his train. Police caught up with him a few days later. Adding insult to injury, McKeown claimed at trial that the sex was consensual. He was wasting his breath.

Dipsh*t analytics for this ex-military marauder:

- **Behavior:** chronic

- **Situation:** benign
- **Cause:** self-Induced
- **Outcome:** 5 (destructive) for McKeown and his victim; (3) disruptive for the property manager and tenants in the building where this crime occurred; 2 (imposing) for the police, prosecutor, and court.

A Hard Way to Go. Coleman McIlvain, age 34, of St. Ann, Missouri is dead – but not soon enough. He shot his girlfriend in the face, then killed her 5-year-old son and her 14-year-old son. A 9-year-old daughter was shot but survived. McIlvain then turned the gun on himself.

Neighbors said the couple fought often and that McIlwain was known to get drunk and fire his gun in the backyard. A relative of the dead woman said she had kicked him out several weeks earlier because of his addiction problems. She let him return when he promised to get his life in order.

According to the young survivor, McIlwain wanted the keys to his girlfriend's car. He'd been drinking, and she refused to let him drive. He then demanded that she drive him. She again refused. He responded by drawing his pistol and shooting her in the face. He then shot her children one by one. McIlwain reportedly had outstanding warrants in Oklahoma.

How many times have we seen this? A mother struggling to raise her children hooks up with an irresponsible and dangerous man. Abuse, addiction, financial exploitation, criminal activity, and other sordid consequences ensue. Sometimes a child is sexually assaulted or killed. In this case, the mother and her children died (except for one traumatized survivor). All the red flags were there. Involve yourself with an obvious dipsh*t at your own peril.

Here's my analysis for the family annihilator:

- **Behavior:** chronic
- **Situation:** provocative (He was drunk and agitated, and she was resisting his demands.)
- **Cause:** habitual (Addiction and criminal history.)
- **Outcome:** 5 (destructive) for the mother, her children, and McIlwain; 3 (disruptive) for the neighborhood; 2 (imposing) for the police, prosecutor, and court.

Unknown Unknowns

When we take on the role of good Samaritan to help a stranger, we probably don't have complete information about the person or situation. That also can be the case even when we aid someone known to us. The man who stopped to help rollover victims on I-94 didn't know they were in a stolen car or that one of the occupants would carjack his vehicle. He saw an emergency and tried to help. Unbeknownst to him, his kindness was about to enable a succession of criminal acts.

Coleman McIlvain's girlfriend, whom he shot point-blank, didn't know he would commit murder-suicide. She certainly knew he was a bad seed, but perhaps she thought he could improve with her help. At worst, she made a terrible mistake. Perhaps she was just too caring for her own good. Even though she knew McIlvain intimately, there were still important things about him she didn't understand (or wouldn't believe).

The familiar adage, "no good deed goes unpunished," warns us to beware of unexpected blowback. When we lack complete information about people or circumstances, hidden risks may be lurking. That's doubly true when dipsh*ts are involved. *The law of unintended consequences* expresses the idea that well-meaning actions can produce undesirable side-effects in addition to the intended results.

Sociologist Robert K. Merton brought the law of unintended consequences to public attention in a journal article published in 1936. He explained that unforeseen consequences may be good, bad, or both. For example, Merton observed that minimum wage laws can simultaneously protect workers and also backfire if employers eliminate jobs or cut working hours to offset their increased expenses. Adam Smith, on the other hand, emphasized only good side-effects in his economic tome, *The Wealth of Nations.* He wrote that the "invisible hand" of the marketplace creates benefits for society (e.g., jobs, new products, innovative services, convenient locations) when investors and entrepreneurs pursue their own profit-driven self-interest.

In the business world, these good, bad, or both consequences are called *externalities.* I have a vivid memory of reading my economics textbook in graduate school when the following sentences stopped me cold: "All businesses generate externalities. Externalities can be either good or bad, but most externalities are bad." I couldn't believe what I'd just read. How could the author categorically declare that most externalities are bad? Had he investigated them all? Then the light bulb went off in my head: Bad externalities (e.g., pollution, traffic congestion caused by new development, etc.) offload companies' problems or expenses onto someone else. Good externalities (e.g., high-paying jobs, carbon-neutral manufacturing) cost companies money. That's why most externalities are bad.

Synonymous with the law of unintended consequences is the *cobra effect*, which owes its name to the following story: When the British ruled India, Delhi was overrun with cobras. To eradicate the snakes, city leaders offered a bounty on cobra skins. At first the program was successful. Skins were turned in for the reward, and the snake population went down. But several enterprising Indians saw an opportunity to maximize profits. They began breeding cobras for their skins.

When the Brits discovered this reproduction scheme, they withdrew the bounty. The breeders, suddenly burdened with unprofitable inventory, set their snakes free. Delhi ended up with a worse cobra problem than before.

Here's a recent example of the cobra effect. The State of Louisiana offers a bounty on nutria, an aquatic mammal resembling a beaver. They have webbed feet and carrot-colored buck teeth. Nutria are cute—and they have been destroying Louisiana's coastal wetlands for years. These pests eat marsh plants down to the roots, which permanently kills the vegetation and hastens erosion.

Hunters are paid $6 per nutria tail in the expectation that the animals will be shot dead. After all, killing them is the point of the bounty program. However, Harris DeHart, age 45, thought he had a better idea. DeHart would catch nutria, cut off their tails, and then release the injured animals back into the swamp. Wildlife and Fisheries agents had no difficulty compiling evidence against him, because this dipsh*t posted videos of his nutria-maiming antics on social media. Not only that, the videos showed him teaching a child to do the same. DeHart was charged with aggravated animal cruelty, illegal hunting, and contributing to the delinquency of a juvenile.

The *savior complex* is another theory that addresses fallout from good intentions. It's a mindset that predisposes a person or group to rescue others from their problems or hardships. This shouldn't be confused with spontaneous rescue attempts, such as pulling someone from a burning building. That's an adrenaline-driven, reflexive reaction. Someone with a savior complex believes, consciously or not, that he or she has superior knowledge or abilities.

The savior complex can prompt a person to presumptuously meddle in the affairs of others. This can generate blowback in countless ways. When a would-be rescuer misjudges the problem, renders unwanted aid or advice, or creates conflict by interfering, that kind of "helping" can easily devolve into dipsh*ttery.

The woman whose phone, car, and dog were stolen by homeless people is a good example of the savior complex gone wrong. She let a homeless man get into her car to warm up. He stole her phone. Then she recruited other homeless people to help track him down. She invited them into the car as well. When she got out, she left the car running. Result: no phone, no car, no dog. This is not the way to help the homeless.

One study found that people were more willing to take risks to save someone's life than to save that person's property. Specifically, the willingness to take risks increased as the severity of the situation increased. Contrary to what you might expect, the greater the danger, the more likely a bystander would act as a good Samaritan. In a less dire situation, the same bystander would feel less pressure to do anything at all. *Arousal theory* suggests that people are more likely to help others when they are in a triggered emotional state, such as fear or excitement. High-risk situations often incite these kinds of emotions and thereby make people more likely to help.

Another reason why people intercede with others in high-risk situations, according to *moral identity theory*, is that they place a high premium on behaving ethically. People with deeply held moral values may feel a stronger sense of obligation to help others, especially when the consequences of not helping are severe. This can motivate people to disregard danger, even if they would not have done so in a low-risk situation. Pat Tillman, a professional football player who abandoned his lucrative career and enlisted in the Army after the 9/11 attacks, exemplifies moral identity theory in practice. (Sadly, Tillman died in Afghanistan from friendly fire.)

One of the paradoxes of trying to help others in crisis is that intervention may be interpreted as hostility. When a good Samaritan's assistance is misinterpreted as an act of aggression by the person in crisis, he or she may react violently. Coleman McIlwain wanted to borrow his girlfriend's car, but she refused because he was drunk. He then demanded that she drive him herself, but she declined to take him anywhere in his inebriated state. Enraged, McIlwain drew his pistol and shot her in the face. Then he shot her children. In her last living act, his girlfriend safeguarded property and lives on the highway. But what McIlwain perceived was defiance.

Murphy's law, as you know, tells us, "Anything that can go wrong will go wrong." But that's just the first law. There are several related laws attributed to Murphy. The fourth law says, "If there is a possibility of several things going wrong, the one that will cause the most damage will be the one to go wrong." A corollary to that law warns that "If there is a worse time for something to go wrong, it will happen then." The fifth law adds, "If anything simply cannot go wrong, it will anyway." Murphy doesn't require a dipsh*t's participation for these laws to hold true. But when one of them does get involved, count on the fallout to leave even Murphy speechless.

High on Heroine

One intrepid lady has found an effective way to bypass the ninth law and intercede effectively with dipsh*ts. I stand in awe of her ingenuity. In fact, I consider her a heroine for our times.

Brandy Williams of Fremont, California noticed missionaries going door to door in her neighborhood. News reports refer to the door-knockers as Jehovah's Witnesses, but they are described as two young men on bicycles. That sounds more like Mormons. Take your pick.

Williams wasn't going to stand idly by and allow this pestilence of proselytizing to go down without a fight. She stripped off her clothes, and when they came to her door, she greeted these comrades of Christ stark naked. The stunned men, named John and Luke (yes, really), froze. But Williams was just getting started.

"Take a look at my p*ssy!" she shouted. "Succumb to my devil vagina magic!" Terrified of this buck-naked vixen and her Satanic lady bits, the holy rollers ran away, jumped on their bikes, and fled. Williams ran down the street after them. For some reason, a woman running nude in the street caught the attention of neighbors. They called the police, and Williams was arrested. A spokesperson for the sheriff's department said the missionaries "are familiar with folks being rude. What Ms. Williams did next went a little too far." If it were up to me, she would receive a commendation for outstanding valor and distinguished service to the community. Go thou and do likewise.

Now to be fair, missionaries have come to my door several times, and I'm never rude to them. But I do send them on their way. I realize they're doing what they think is good and right. In a world brimming over with dipsh*ts, I respect that even though I don't want them bothering me. I just couldn't resist having a bit of fun by praising Williams' shenanigans.

In 21st century America, where people have been shot for knocking on the wrong door or pulling into the wrong driveway, religious proselytizers should count themselves fortunate if all they get are doors slammed in their faces. Every residence they approach amounts to "the triumph of hope over experience" as far as personal safety is concerned. But that's moral identity theory in practice. Their personal identity and their faith are so intertwined that they feel duty-bound to convert others.

The moral of the Williams story (if there is one) is that you'd best strip off your clothes, do the hokey-pokey, or otherwise confuse and overwhelm whomever you're about to intervene with if you expect to emerge unscathed. That's doubly true when you're dealing with noxious miscreants. But most of us probably don't have Williams' zeal. Even so, "Devil Vagina Magic" would be a great name for a rock band.

* * *

"Whenever a man does a thoroughly stupid thing, it is always from the noblest motives."
– Oscar Wilde

Chapter Eleven

The Tenth Law: Dipsh*ttery is a Force of Nature Which Can Neither be Eradicated nor Avoided

In the early 1880s an Irish lass, Mary Mallon, emigrated to the United States in search of a better life. She settled in New York and held a succession of jobs as a cook in private homes. In 1900, when Mallon worked for the Warren family of Long Island, several members of that household fell ill with typhoid fever, a highly contagious and potentially deadly disease caused by the bacterium *Salmonella typhi*. It was to be the beginning of an epidemic, but Mallon never came down with typhoid herself.

Mallon was hired as a cook for the Thompsons in 1901. Again, several family members came down with the fever. She held that job until 1904 when the Colemans hired her as their cook. Typhoid struck them as well. The patten continued with the Bowen family, who hired her in 1906, and the Browns who employed her in 1907. Everywhere Mallon worked, sickness followed.

The Thompsons hired George Soper, a sanitary engineer, to ferret out the cause of the outbreak that had so devastated their loved ones. He gathered information about the family, people who worked in the household or visited the residence, and commonalities between the Thompsons and other afflicted families.

Mallon emerged as the common denominator. When he tested samples of Mallon's cooking, he discovered the lurking typhoid bacterium.

Soper notified public health officials of his findings. They ordered Mallon's detainment for physical examination and testing. She was outraged at accusations that she was a carrier of the disease. She refused to accept any responsibility and claimed she was being singled out for persecution because she was an Irish immigrant. Mallon insisted that she be allowed to live her life and continue working. Once it became clear that she would continue spreading typhoid if left alone, authorities took drastic action. In 1907, she was quarantined against her will on North Brother Island in the East River, where she remained until her death in 1938.

Remembered in history as "Typhoid Mary," Mallon exemplifies the principle that dipsh*ttery cannot be eradicated from society, nor can we completely avoid it. Why? Because dipsh*ts en masse would have to cease behaving stupidly and despicably. It's up to them to fix their behavior. How likely is that?

Let's do dipsh*t analytics on Typhoid Mary:

- **Behavior:** chronic
- **Situation:** provocative (Her situation was benign until she was confronted with the evidence of her carrier status. Then life became provocative for her.)
- **Cause:** triggered (By her diagnosis.)
- **Outcome:** 5 (destructive) for those infected by Mallon, their families, and Typhoid Mary herself; 3 (disruptive) for

George Soper, public health officials, and staff at the facility where she was confined.

Consider the case of "V.N.," a Tacoma, Washington woman whose identity is protected by court order. She was arrested in June 2023 for being a carrier of tuberculosis. Despite a year-long attempt by health department officials to convince her to seek treatment or isolate herself, the woman stubbornly refused. She defied court orders, and a judge finally issued a warrant for her arrest. A health department official testified that, despite all their warnings and entreaties, he saw V.N. get on a bus and travel to a casino. That seems to have been the straw that broke the tubercular camel's back.

Sheriff's deputies arrested V.N. and transported her to jail in a vehicle rigged to prevent her infectious breath from migrating to the front seat from the back. A "negative pressure" cell, which prevents air from escaping, awaited her. It was equipped with medical devices and supplies to enable treatment and testing. Seventeen court hearings, hundreds of hours of effort by public health officials, and forcible incarceration were necessary to prevent the deadly behavior of one dipsh*t determined to follow in the steps of Mary Mallon.

Dipsh*t analytics for V.N. (Very Noxious):

- **Behavior:** chronic
- **Situation:** benign (Unlike Typhoid Mary, she had many opportunities to accept treatment and lead a relatively normal life.)
- **Cause:** self-induced

- **Outcome:** 4 (damaging) for V.N. and her family (her confinement will be temporary); 5 (destructive) for anyone she infected; 3 (disruptive) for public health officials, the sheriff's department, and the court.

In the United States, we saw countless "mini-Mallons" flouting social distancing, masking, quarantine, and vaccination protocols during COVID-19. Many of these were people who didn't understand, didn't believe, or didn't care that they could spread the disease even though they were symptom-free. Much of this defiance was politically driven.

If you think it's outrageous for infectious patients to act in flagrant disregard of public health, consider how reprehensible it is when a physician does it. A case in point is the plastic surgeon in Ohio who lost her medical license because of her outrageous behavior.

Dr. Katharine Roxanne Grawe, age 44, cultivated a social media following by livestreaming herself on Tik Tok while performing surgery. In 2018, the State Medical Board of Ohio warned her that such conduct compromised patients' privacy and raised ethical concerns, KBZK-TV reported. And yet Grawe, known to her followers as "Dr. Roxy," persisted. In fact, she was reprimanded twice according to CNN.

Finally, the State Medical Board took enforcement action in November 2022. They barred Grawe from practicing medicine, but as a matter of due process, she was granted a hearing to appeal the decision. In July 2023 she appeared before the board and gave heartfelt testimony that she had seen the error of her ways. Grawe "complained about the impact the accusations against her had on her life outside of the office as she said her kids have been attacked in school and her husband left her," *USA Today* reported. She said that she never thought she'd be subjected to this level of punishment.

The board members seemed especially concerned that recordings of Grawe's livestreamed operations showed her looking away from the patient and responding to questions from her followers. At least four women filed lawsuits against her for injuries alleged to have occurred during these publicly shared surgeries. KBZK-TV reported:

> According to the board's notice, one unnamed patient had to be hospitalized days after receiving a tummy tuck, Brazilian butt-lift, and liposuction because she had a perforated small bowel and a soft tissue infection. A second patient was also found to have six intestinal cuts and multiple tears in the bowel wall, which required the removal of a part of the small intestine and partial removal of abdominal tissue.
>
> The third unnamed patient mentioned in the notice received a breast augmentation with silicone implants. Days later, the patient complained of bleeding from her chest. She was then hospitalized for having a faster than normal heart rate. A general surgeon had to operate and remove a hematoma from her breasts, along with the implants.

Someone created a private Facebook group, entitled "Enough Is Enough. Have You Been a Victim of Dr. Roxy?" in the wake of Grawe's license suspension. Women have shared their experiences there, including one woman who told the station she didn't think Grawe should get her license back, WSYX-TV stated.

Grawe's appeal before the State Medical Board failed. They wrote that her "continued practice presents a danger of immediate and serious harm to the public." She was also fined $4,500.00. No information is available about the status of patients' litigation against her.

How many times does an intelligent, educated, experienced physician need to be told that what she's doing will likely result in serious consequences for her patients and herself? In fact, why must she be warned at all? I've taught at universities that offer nursing programs. I know of instances when nursing students were kicked out of the program for taking photos or videos of patients' injuries or illnesses, even though the individuals weren't named, and their faces weren't shown. Even nursing students are taught not to compromise patients' privacy and suffer unforgiving punishment if they do.

Dipsh*t analytics for Doctor Tik Tok:

- **Behavior:** hybrid (Grawe's social media antics seem to have affected only one area of her life – i.e., her surgical practice.)
- **Situation:** benign (Operations are stressful for patients, at least until they're anesthetized. Normally, I'd assume operations to be frenetic even for a surgeon, but not for one who felt comfortable enough to livestream and answer viewers' questions.)
- **Cause:** self-induced
- **Outcome:** 5 (destructive) for injured patients and their families and for Grawe and her family; 4 (damaging) for any medical staff who worked for Grawe and lost their jobs because of her suspension from practice; (4) damaging for any hospital where she performed surgeries, if they were

also named as defendants by Grawe's patients; 2 (imposing) for members of the State Medical Board.

Contagious patients and dangerous doctors aren't the only people who illustrate the tenth law's proposition that dipsh*ttery is, was, and always will be with us. A common theme in the cases of Mallon, V.N., and Grawe is their stubborn and irresponsible refusal to heed warnings from experts. Here are some additional cases from outside the medical realm that manifest the same arrogant dismissiveness and blithe disregard of risk to others.

Six-shooter. A six-year-old in Newport News, Virginia brought a gun to school and shot his first-grade teacher in the face. It was no accident. The boy had a well-documented "history of random violence that required special interventions on a daily basis," WLS-TV reported. By the grace of God, that teacher, Abigail Zwerner, survived and has filed a $40 million lawsuit against the school district.

The boy's parents told reporters that their son "suffers from an acute disability and was under a care plan at the school that included his mother or father attending school with him and accompanying him to class every day." But both parents were absent on the day Zwerner was shot. Two days earlier, this tiny terror had grabbed Zwerner's phone and smashed it. She called a school security officer, who reportedly did not respond.

In her lawsuit, Zwerner alleges that she told Ebony Parker, an assistant principal, "that the boy was in a 'violent mood,' had threatened to beat up a kindergartner during lunchtime and 'angrily stared down a security officer in the lunchroom.' The suit alleges that the assistant principal took no action and even refused to look at Zwerner when she expressed concern," according to WLS-TV. Later, some students told a teacher that the boy had a gun. When Parker was notified, she dismissed the matter by saying the child's "pockets were too small to hold a handgun and did nothing," WLS-TV reported.

In the wake of this debacle, the superintendent was fired, and Ebony Parker resigned. The feral first-grader cannot be charged with a crime, because he is deemed unable at his age to form criminal intent within the legal definition. His mother, however, was indicted. Deja Taylor was charged with felony child neglect and one count of recklessly leaving a firearm accessible to her son. She pleaded guilty in June 2023 and is awaiting sentencing. She faces up to five years in prison for the felony child neglect charge and up to one year in jail for the misdemeanor charge. No charges were brought against the boy's father.

Dipsh*t analytics for those who turned deaf ears to the warnings:

- **Behavior:** chronic
- **Situation:** provocative
- **Cause:** self-induced
- **Outcome:** 5 (destructive) for Zwerner and her family as well as the boy and his family; 4 (damaging) for the people who lost their jobs and for the students, faculty, and staff at that school; 3 (disruptive) for social services personnel who must deal with the boy's emotional and behavioral problems; 3 (disruptive) for the school board; 2 (imposing) for the police, prosecutor, and court.

Dipsh*t analytics for the boy's mother, who allegedly left a gun within his reach:

- **Behavior:** chronic
- **Situation:** frenetic (Parenting a child with severe behavioral issues is probably frenetic most of the time, so I'm going with that.)
- **Cause:** habitual (Possibly self-induced, but when guns are left around children, I take this to indicate persistent dipsh*ttery.)
- **Outcome:** 5 (destructive) for that entire family and for Zwerner and her family; 4 (damaging) for the school, its students, and employees; 3 (disruptive) for the school board; 2 (imposing) for police, prosecutor, and the court.

That's a Rap. Have you ever been in a crowd so densely packed that you couldn't move or breathe? I've never been unable to breathe in a crowd, but at Mardi Gras years ago, I had the frightening experience of being carried along by the momentum of the mob, unable to escape. If I had fallen, I would have been trampled. People attending the 2021 Astroworld Festival in Houston, Texas had a worse experience than mine. Some people said they were so tightly compressed that they couldn't breathe. They were the lucky ones.

The festival, founded by rapper Travis Scott, struggled with crowd control from the outset. On the night of Scott's performance, chaos erupted. Non-paying gatecrashers broke through the perimeter and stormed the stage. This onslaught, combined with the surge of ticketed attendees, created a spontaneous stampede. People were trampled, ten of whom died, including a 9-year-old boy who had to be placed in a medically induced coma.

Despite seeing this debacle unfold from his vantage point on the stage, Scott did not stop the show or call for order. It was during his performance that the deadly mayhem commenced, and lawsuits filed afterwards allege that he incited the crowd. Live Nation, another defendant in the lawsuits, stands accused of failing to provide effective crowd management and adequate security.

Dipsh*t analytics for Scott and festival promoters:

- **Behavior:** chronic
- **Situation:** provocative (An onrushing mob of intruders combined with the rowdy jostling of the ticketed attendees.)
- **Cause:** habitual (When someone organizes a public event and either doesn't know how to plan appropriate crowd control or doesn't care to, that's incompetence based on an abundance of bad decisions.)
- **Outcome:** 5 (destructive) for those who were killed and their families; 4 (damaging) for attendees who were injured and for their families; 3 (disruptive) for festival-goers who were caught in the crowd surge and feared for their safety; 4 (damaging) for Scott and festival promoters who now face legal challenges.

Faulty Towers. In June 2021 the Champlain Towers South condominium in Surfside, Florida collapsed. It was to become one of the deadliest building implosions in U.S. history. Recovery efforts took several weeks, and 98 people were confirmed dead. An unknown number were injured, and countless pets also died amid the rubble.

Prior to the collapse, there were repeated warnings about the building's apparent deterioration. A 2018 engineering report commissioned by the condominium association identified areas of major damage as well as degradation of the concrete slab under the pool deck and entrance driveway. The report warned of "major structural damage" that would "exponentially" increase repair costs if not promptly repaired. Residents likewise pointed out cracks and other visible signs of damage. Some had expressed concerns about the safety and structural integrity of the building.

The condominium association did seek bids for repairing the structural problems. In April 2021 the board passed a special assessment that detailed the necessary renovation and its associated costs. The assessment included a timeline for completing the repair work. However, the collapse occurred before significant progress could be made. The exact cause is still under investigation, and it's unclear whether the authorized repairs, if completed, would have prevented the tragedy.

The Champlain Towers South collapse is doubly tragic because the condo board recognized that structural problems existed and took action to address them. Their efforts were both futile and wasted because they proceeded in a slow and deliberative manner. They accepted the reality of major defects, but they didn't heed the engineering report's emphasis that urgency was required (perhaps because they lacked sufficient reserve funds to complete the repairs until revenue from the special assessment was collected). Previous condo boards, however, had allowed the building to deteriorate by deferring maintenance and repairs.

Dipsh*t analytics for the succession of condo boards who allowed the damage to accumulate:

- **Behavior:** chronic
- **Situation:** benign (No one in charge seemed alarmed enough about the problems for the situation be deemed frenetic or provocative.)
- **Cause:** habitual (Deferred maintenance and repairs, year after year.)
- **Outcome:** 5 (destructive) for those who died, their families, and for everyone whose condo was destroyed by the collapse; 4 (destructive) for adjacent properties; 3 (disruptive) for the local community and city government; 2 (disruptive) for first responders and recovery crews.

Smooth, Crunchy, or Tainted. In 2008 the Peanut Corporation of America (PCA) knowingly sold contaminated peanut butter and other peanut-related products to the American public. The company was aware of salmonella within its processing facilities but failed to take corrective action or inform regulators. As a result, tainted peanut butter made its way onto store shelves and into the shopping baskets of consumers nationwide.

Nine people died of salmonella poisoning contracted from PCA's spoiled products. The Centers for Disease Control reported that more than 700 were sickened, but there may have been many more unreported cases. It was one of the largest outbreaks of foodborne illness in U.S. history. Inspections of PCA's facilities uncovered rodent and insect infestation, mold, dirt, and debris. Both the roasting equipment and water system tested positive for salmonella.

Several corporate officers were convicted and sentenced for their collusion in the sale of the poisonous products. Among these was Stewart Parnell, who served as the CEO of PCA at the time of the contamination. He was found guilty of multiple charges in 2014, including conspiracy, fraud, and introduction of adulterated food into interstate commerce. He was held responsible for knowingly allowing toxic peanut products to be sold, despite being aware of the health risks they posed. In 2015, Parnell was sentenced to 28 years in prison, the harshest penalty ever given for a food safety violation.

Besides Parnell, two other individuals associated with the PCA were convicted for their roles in the scandal. Michael Parnell, Stewart's brother, was a food broker who worked with PCA. He was found guilty of conspiracy, fraud, and other charges and received a 20-year prison sentence. Mary Wilkerson, the quality control manager at PCA's Blakely, Georgia facility, was also convicted. She was found guilty of obstruction of justice for intentionally destroying documents related to the contamination. Wilkerson was sentenced to five years in prison.

PCA faced numerous lawsuits and claims for damages from individuals, businesses, and organizations affected by the tainted peanut products. The company also hemorrhaged customers in the wake of the food poisoning scandal. The combination of legal challenges and declining product sales proved fatal for the company. PCA filed for bankruptcy and went out of business.

Stewart Parnell approved the distribution of products that PCA's own internal testing had indicated were contaminated with salmonella. He reportedly ordered the tests to be run again until the samples passed. As CEO, Parnell had the power to remedy the sanitation problems and to halt the shipment of dangerous food. He's the one person who could have saved lives, saved the company, and saved himself from prison.

Dipsh*t analytics for the Parnells and Wilkerson:

- **Behavior:** chronic
- **Situation:** benign
- **Cause:** habitual
- **Outcome:** 5 (destructive) for consumers who were killed by the toxic products and for their families; 5 (destructive) for the incarcerated PCA officials and their families; 4 (damaging) for people who were sickened by salmonella and also their families; 4 (damaging) for PCA employees who lost their jobs when the company went bankrupt; 3 (disruptive) for health officials who had to track the source of the salmonella poisonings and who had to inspect PCA's filthy facilities; 2 (imposing) for the police, prosecutor, and court.

So, reckless and irresponsible people ignore warnings and disregard obvious signs of risk. What a shock. Stupefying behavior often seems perfectly reasonable to the person committing the jaw-dropping malfeasance, however. Other than good, old-fashioned denial, what might account for their incomprehensible actions?

Don't Worry, Be Happy

In her book, *The Optimism Bias: A Tour of the Irrationally Positive Brain*, psychologist Tali Sharot explained how individuals tend to underestimate their chances of experiencing negative events while overestimating their chances of experiencing positive events. *Optimism bias* is the belief that one is less likely to suffer adverse outcomes compared to others. Sharot's research indicates that people are prone to this cognitive error in many aspects of life, such as health, finances, and personal safety.

For example, Stockton Rush, the CEO of OceanGate Expeditions, repeatedly dismissed warnings from experts that the company's Titan submersible was at risk of failure at ocean depths. He blithely assured one potential customer that the sub was "safer than crossing the street." (Well, maybe if you're crossing in Pamplona during the running of the bulls.) His devil-may-care attitude heralded doom for himself, his passengers, and perhaps for the company as well.

Ebony Parker, the assistant principal, who dismissed reports that an unruly child had a gun, may have believed (as she reportedly said) that his pockets were too small to conceal a pistol. Based on that, she may have concluded that nothing bad would happen. Stewart Parnell of PCA might have assumed that a few germs in food wouldn't hurt anyone. The condo board at Champlain Towers South possibly concluded that the damage would wait until they got around to repairing it. "*What's the rush? It's not like the building's going to fall down because of some cracks in the concrete.*"

Diffusion of responsibility also may have influenced the condominium board. This theory suggests that individuals may ignore warnings and take risks when they believe that responsibility is shared among a group. Each person may assume that someone else will take appropriate action and so no one takes the initiative. Another possibility is that the board may have lapsed into *groupthink*. If a voting member observes that others on the board believe deferring repairs is appropriate, he or she may go along despite having reservations.

When Travis Scott was on stage during the Astroworld Festival, he could see the chaos unfolding before him. But he was in the middle of a set. Even though he organized the event, he might have assumed that crowd control was not his concern. Let the security personnel and police handle it. That too is diffusion of responsibility.

Another reason why people foolishly disregard warnings and looming risks is because they believe they've already done enough to prepare. OceanGate's CEO certainly thought he had taken enough precautions. *Risk homeostasis theory* suggests that people have a set level of risk they are comfortable with, and that they will adjust their behavior to maintain that level of risk. For example, if a motorcyclist feels safer wearing a helmet, he or she may ride faster or closer to traffic. On the other hand, someone driving a car during rush hour traffic and in heavy fog will adjust by being more alert and cautious than usual.

It's possible that Stewart Parnell, as CEO of PCA, felt protected from the consequences of shipping contaminated food. He may have concluded that no one would get sick, and even if they did, that he would be untouchable. If he felt safe, this could explain his orders to ship tainted products. Similarly, "Dr. Roxy," the livestreaming plastic surgeon, may have felt that she could ignore the State Medical Board's warnings and still keep her license to practice. Both Parnell and Grawe discovered the hard way that their sense of security was illusory.

Sometimes people feel entitled to just do whatever they want to do. We may think of such people as narcissistic, selfish, arrogant, or even evil. While those characterizations can be true if an individual behaves that way consistently, there are other explanations for occasional bad conduct. *Moral licensing theory* indicates that people may commit morally dubious acts after behaving in a virtuous manner. Their benevolent acts can make people feel entitled to misbehave in contradiction to their previously righteous behavior. It's a way of balancing their moral self-image. Think of the Catholic priests who have aided the needy, comforted the sick, consoled the grieving, ministered to the sinful – and yet have sexually abused altar boys.

Surely "Dr. Roxy" must have helped and healed many people before tanking her medical career. Stewart Parnell was a Baptist and served on many industry boards and committees before releasing poison peanut butter into the marketplace. People who want to engage in illicit behavior can avoid cognitive dissonance by rationalizing: *"I'm really a good person because of all the things I do for others, so I'm allowed to bend the rules now and then."* Remember Ted Haggard, the drug-using, philandering megachurch pastor? He reportedly rationalized that he could sow his wild oats as long as he also prayed and fasted. That's moral licensing in a nutshell.

Whatever Floats Your Boat

Donald Crowhurst was a British businessman and amateur sailor who decided it would be great fun to enter the Sunday Times Golden Globe Race, a single-handed, around-the-world yacht race held in 1968–69. Crowhurst had limited sailing experience. He had captained small boats in the English Channel, but he had never sailed on a large ocean-going vessel. He also had no experience with single-handed sailing. The race was a long and challenging journey, and Crowhurst lacked mechanical skills to repair his boat if it broke down.

Armed with supreme over-confidence, this dipsh*t mariner set about building a custom trimaran himself. When it was finished, several sailors and experts warned Crowhurst that his boat, the *Teignmouth Electron*, was not seaworthy. They pointed out that, at 48 feet long, the boat was too small and that it was not properly sealed. Crowhurst's lack of experience was also pointed out to him.

Nevertheless, when race day arrived, Crowhurst set out with the others. It wasn't long before his boat began taking on water. He was forced to fix structural damage, which slowed him down and gave his competitors a head start. To create the illusion of keeping up, Crowhurst began to fake his positions. He would send radio reports that made it seem like he was making good progress, when actually he was sailing in circles in the Atlantic Ocean. The situation was hopeless, but he did not turn back.

Crowhurst persisted in the deception for several months. He sent radio reports that made it seem as though he was nearing the finish line. In reality, he was nowhere near. He even faked a radio conversation with his wife, Vivienne. His lies were exposed in July 1969, when his boat was found abandoned in the Atlantic. Crowhurst's body was never found, and his death is still a mystery. Some have speculated that he died by suicide, while others believe he either abandoned his boat or was washed overboard. Crowhurst's story has been the subject of several books and films, including the 2007 film *The Mercy* starring Colin Firth. It's a story that continues to fascinate and intrigue people today.

Crowhurst's decision to fake his positions was probably motivated by a combination of factors, including financial pressure, fear of failure, and a desire to achieve glory. He ignored warnings, overestimated his sailing abilities, and underestimated the unforgiving nature of the sea. His stubbornness was such that he chose to risk his life rather than admit failure and turn back.

Unlike the other cases in this chapter, Captain Dipsh*t only harmed himself and his family. But like Typhoid Mary and V.N., someone would have had to forcibly restrain him to prevent his sailing into oblivion. Dipsh*ttery can't be eradicated or avoided, as the tenth law informs us, because we can't lock them all up.

Here are the analytics for Donald "Voyage to the Bottom of the Sea" Crowhurst:

- **Behavior:** chronic
- **Situation:** benign
- **Cause:** habitual (There's some evidence that Crowhurst was a reckless and financially troubled individual.)
- **Outcome:** 5 (destructive) for Crowhurst and his family; 3 (disruptive) for rescuers searching for him.

How could Crowhurst not see the danger and weigh his limited skills against the momentous challenges ahead? Impulsivity theory, as you'll recall from chapter five, indicates that some people are prone to reckless behavior due to genetics, brain chemistry, or environmental influences. They may be incapable of understanding risk until it's too late. Even past catastrophes may not deter them, because they do not retain the lessons learned from previous mistakes.

Crowhurst borrowed large sums from friends and family to finance his boat even though he had no means to repay the money if he didn't win the race. He built his boat by himself without professional help, resulting in a craft that was unseaworthy. And here's the icing on this rancid cake: He told his wife and children that he was leaving on a business trip when in fact he was setting off on a months-long and ultimately fatal quixotic adventure. You can always tell a dipsh*t, but you can't tell him much.

* * *

"Nothing in all the world is more dangerous than sincere ignorance and conscientious stupidity."
– Martin Luther King, Jr.

Chapter Twelve

Against Dipsh*ts the Very Gods Contend in Vain

The maxim, "Against stupidity the very gods contend in vain," comes from Act III, Scene VI of Friedrich Schiller's play *The Maid of Orleans* (*Die Jungfrau von Orleans*). It appears again in Arthur Schopenhauer's *Parerga and Paralipomena* (1851) with Schiller credited as the source. This timeless observation expresses the frustration we feel when trying to talk sense to people who are stubbornly ignorant and impervious to reason or evidence. It's doubly true when we struggle to engage rationally with dipsh*ts.

That many such people hold positions of power in governments, militaries, churches, corporations, universities, and other institutions is a regrettable fact of life. Ensconced where they can do maximum harm, they blithely sow incompetence, irresponsibility, and ignorance on a mass scale. For example, "military intelligence" is often cited as an oxymoron – sometimes by rank-and-file service members themselves. Consider the following example from the annals (anals?) of recent history.

Shortly after the U.S. invaded Iraq in the wake of 9/11, the Defense Department purchased "bomb detectors" from ATSC, Ltd. (Advanced Tactical Security & Communication Limited), a British company. James McCormick, the firm's founder and managing director, presented two devices, the ADE651 and

GT200, as revolutionary technological innovations based on "ion mobility spectrometry" that could sense and locate explosives. These hand-held detectors had an antenna that swiveled and pointed in the direction of concealed bombs. That was McCormick's story, anyway.

American military brass thought these high-tech gadgets sounded pretty good and bought $40 million worth of them. Now, I know what you're thinking: Surely the government tested these products before buying them. Yes and no, they did and they didn't, as the case may be. I hope that clarifies the matter for you.

Here's what happened: ATSC, Ltd. was allowed to set up controlled demonstrations for Pentagon officials. These product tests were orchestrated in a way that allowed the devices to seemingly detect hidden explosives. However, the testing methodology lacked scientific validity and was carefully manipulated to deceive potential buyers. The company supplied misleading documentation and promotional material, including testimonials and reports, supposedly verifying the effectiveness of the detectors. However, these materials were not peer reviewed and contained fabricated or cherry-picked data to support the false claims.

Another way McCormick's company bamboozled military officers was by using opaque and pseudoscientific jargon, such as "ion diffusion," "electrostatic fields," and "substance specific resonance." The company also preyed on urgency and fear of terrorist attacks and bombings that could (and did) kill troops in Iraq. ATSC, Ltd. hammered home the message that their bogus devices were essential for saving lives.

As you've already deduced, McCormick's bomb detectors were fraudulent devices. They consisted of nothing more than a plastic box with a microchip and motor inside that caused the antenna to swivel in random directions. The Pentagon might as well have bought $40 million dollars' worth of Ouija boards.

Not only did the non-detectors fail to find concealed bombs (except by chance), but they also randomly implicated innocent people. A 2014 study by the BBC concluded that, because of these useless gadgets, 1,000 people or more may have died in Iraq from undetected explosives. But ATSC, Ltd. also sold their pseudo-detectors to governments of many other nations. So the toll of dead and injured directly attributable to McCormick's company is unknown.

Once technical experts got their hands on the devices and took them apart, the scheme unraveled. It took a while for that to happen, because ATSC, Ltd. warned that opening the plastic case would void the warranty. The U.S. finally woke up and stopped distributing the faux detectors in Iraq in 2011, but there is evidence that some remained in use until 2014.

In January 2010 British authorities arrested James McCormick on charges of fraud and deception for knowingly promoting and selling ineffective devices to governments and security forces worldwide. He went on trial in 2013 and was convicted of having willfully deceived governments and organizations, leading to the loss of lives and significant financial costs. The judge sentenced McCormick to 10 years, calling his actions a "callous confidence trick."

McCormick is a swindler and a dipsh*t, but he's insignificant in comparison to the gaggle of civilian and military bureaucrats who allowed this deadly flim-flam to go down without any direct, first-hand, unbiased testing under battlefield conditions. *Forty million dollars* – you'd think they would buy just two or three at first and see if they actually worked before showering ATSC, Ltd. with cash. It might have been cheaper for the United States just to pay the terrorists not to bomb anybody.

I won't prepare a dipsh*t analysis for the Pentagon's fake bomb detectors fiasco, nor will I do so for any of the institutional dipsh*ts in this chapter. There are a couple of reasons for this. First, dipsh*t analytics is intended for evaluation of individuals, not organizational entities. Second, not everyone at the Pentagon or in this chapter's other cases deserves to be criticized for the actions of a few within the organization. By now, you're quite capable of applying dipsh*t analytics yourself if you want to practice on these conglomerated cretins.

Governments and militaries, of course, are not alone in committing institutional dipsh*ttery. The American Red Cross (ARC), widely admired and respected for its disaster relief services and blood drives, has a lesser-known history of scandal. What are we to conclude when one sordid episode after another embroils the organization? (Oops, I did it again?)

From the mid-1980s until the early 1990s, the ARC failed to adequately screen donated blood for HIV/AIDS. Thousands of patients who received blood transfusions during this period caught the deadly disease and lost their lives. This crisis hit very close to home for me.

For several years during the 1980s, I was executive director of the Louisiana Chapter of the National Hemophilia Foundation. I don't have a bleeding disorder myself, but I knew many patients and their families. People with hemophilia and related disorders must take injections of "clotting factor concentrate," which is derived from donated blood. Tainted blood during the 1980s and 1990s decimated this population, leaving their loved ones devastated. But let's move on. We have a lot of ground to cover with the ARC.

After the World Trade Center attacks on September 11 2001, Americans and others from around the world donated an astounding $1.1 billion to the ARC for relief to the families of those who were killed. First responders, people in lower Manhattan who couldn't return home, employees who lost their jobs, and locals requiring mental health counseling were also in need of financial assistance. Within the first month alone, about $543 million was pledged to the "Liberty Fund," which the ARC set up to receive donations specifically for 9/11 relief. But during that month, when panic and terror were at their height, less than one-third of that amount was distributed. Meanwhile, the ARC held about $250,000 in reserve. This foot-dragging led to an outcry from both the public and the media that, as an emergency relief organization, the ARC was not acting with urgency. This naturally led to scrutiny of the charity's overall stewardship.

In 2001 the ARC expended only about 56 cents of every dollar on direct aid to victims. The remainder went to administrative expenses, overhead, and fundraising. Bernadine Healy, president of the organization at that time, drew scorn for her $495,000 salary (later reduced to a mere $425,000). To its credit, the ARC made several changes intended to improve financial controls and to speed distribution of aid. The scandals did not end, however.

Along came Hurricane Katrina in 2005, devastating New Orleans and the Gulf Coast region. Again, the nation and the world opened their wallets to the ARC. But the organization didn't begin distributing funds to victims until about six months after the storm. Even then, the maximum grant for home rebuilding was only $1,500. And once again, critics blasted the organization for its operating costs. About 30 cents for every dollar donated for flood victims went to overhead expenses.

See if you detect a pattern: In 2012 Superstorm Sandy ravaged the Eastern coast of the United States. The ARC sprang into action, once again demonstrating its inimitable efficiency in raking in cash. President Obama appealed to the nation on behalf of Sandy victims for donations to the charity. As always, people responded generously. But the organization's own employees and documents reveal an emphasis on image over substance. National Public Radio (NPR) reported:

> Multiple internal documents obtained by NPR and ProPublica along with interviews with top Red Cross officials reveal an organization that struggled to meet the basic needs of victims in the first weeks after the storm. The documents and interviews also depict an organization so consumed with public relations that it hindered the charity's ability to provide disaster services.
>
> . . .
>
> The Red Cross national headquarters in Washington "diverted assets for public relations purposes." A former Red Cross official

managing the Sandy effort says 40 percent of available trucks were assigned to serve as backdrops for news conferences.

. . .

In one shelter, "sex offenders were...all over, including playing in children's area," according to a confidential "lessons learned" memo from the Red Cross.

Casey Stengel, former manager of the New York Mets, is famous for saying, "Can't anybody here play this game?" He was frustrated by his team's lack of prowess with ball, bat, and glove. Stengel's exasperated query seems equally applicable to the ARC. If insanity is doing the same thing over and over and expecting different results, then dipsh*ttery is making the same mistakes over and over and not taking steps to avoid them in the future.

If you think I'm being too hard on the ARC, then you should know there are several other scandals I haven't mentioned. If I were to continue chronicling the organization's shortcomings, there would be space for nothing else in this chapter. Clara Barton founded the ARC in 1881 as a grassroots volunteer organization. In 1905 Congress chartered the ARC as the country's national disaster relief agency. The venerated charity has been around long enough (in Casey Stengel's words) to "know how to play this game." For the good that they do, Americans are grateful. But considering the amount of money they receive, surely the public is entitled to more than haphazardness and mediocrity.

Another source of premium dipsh*ttery is higher education. I'm a retired professor, and I loved my profession. But that doesn't make me blind to stupid and despicable behavior. Here's an example I witnessed first-hand.

For a couple of years I taught at a small, private college in the Midwest. I wanted to stay longer, but the events I'm about to relay prevented that. The school had two academic tracks – daytime classes for traditional college students and an evening track for working adults who wanted to earn a degree. I taught in both the day and evening programs, with the evening track comprising about fifteen percent of my salary.

The night classes for working adults had seen a steady dropoff in enrollment in recent years. This was due in no small part to the college's miserly $15,000 annual budget to advertise the evening program. During the time I taught at that school, my night classes sometimes had as few as six students and never more than ten. Enrollment that low is not economically sustainable.

The college president decreed that the evening program would end in one year unless enrollment drastically increased. He was allocating the usual $15,000 marketing budget to accomplish this miracle. And what he did next was so fatal to the program that they might as well have set fire to the money. At least they could have had a nice bonfire and marshmallow roast.

In a stunningly dipsh*t move, the president gave the marketing budget to our finance and accounting professor and told him to do his best to save the program. My office was next to that professor's – and I was the advertising and marketing professor. (I have an MBA in addition to my doctorate in psychology.) Not only that, before coming to higher education, I marketed my start-up company nationwide, eventually expanding into 14 states. The finance and accounting professor understood the mathematics and economics of money, but not advertising, promotion, and public relations.

Bear with me for a moment as I present a mini-tutorial on marketing. First, nothing in advertising or marketing should be undertaken without identifying the target audience, understanding their needs and wants, and then strategically planning a campaign to address the audience and their interests. When advertising is done tactically – "let's try some radio spots and see if they work" or "I heard that direct mail is effective, so let's use that" – it's amateurish and wasteful. Second, people need to encounter a marketing message three to ten times across different media for it to "stick" in their minds and for them to respond. With a $15,000 budget, it's impossible to reach the entire audience that many times, so the best option would be to reach a portion of that audience the required number of times, employing different media channels. Reaching the entire audience fewer than three times would be money thrown away.

There's much more one would need to know, of course, but you can see that it takes planning and know-how for marketing to achieve results. The finance and accounting professor didn't know these things – but I did and I was right next door. Rather than consulting me, he went to the college's two-person PR and marketing department, staffed by a couple of young social media nerds. They advised him to spend the entire $15,000 on Facebook ads. When I heard this, I cringed. And I began applying for faculty positions at other schools. I knew from this fact alone that the evening program was doomed. And I wasn't going to accept a fifteen percent pay cut because of the college's mismanagement.

Sure enough, enrollment dropped off to nothing that final year. I moved on to a university that promoted me to associate professor and appointed me as dean. Instead of a pay cut, I got a pay raise. Again and again in higher education, I witnessed smart people making stupid and despicable decisions outside their areas of expertise.

The college president gave the $15,000 marketing budget to the finance and accounting professor because that individual had been with the college for many years. I was new to the college that year. But longevity of employment is irrelevant to one's ability to do a specific job. The president should have chosen someone with task-specific knowledge and skill – which would have been me in this case – rather than an unqualified employee with seniority. Instead, of saving the program, the president ensured its destruction. He meant well, but he didn't know what he was doing.

As a final example of institutional malfeasance, consider the sexual scandals of the Southern Baptist Convention (SBC). The Catholic Church's molestation epidemic is more widely publicized, and for that reason most people are already aware of priestly prurience. I won't rehash that sordid history. But in the U.S., the SBC is second only to Catholicism in membership, and the problems within that denomination are egregious.

In 2018 the *Houston Chronicle* and the *San Antonio Express-News* published an investigative report that exposed hundreds of cases of sexual abuse and misconduct within SBC churches over the previous two decades. Over 700 victims came forward, and more than 400 Southern Baptist church leaders and volunteers were implicated in the abuse, according to the newspapers' reports. Here are few examples:

- In 1998 Claude Thomas Eady Jr., pastor of a Pasadena, Texas SBC church, was accused of sexually abusing a 14-year-old girl. However, rather than reporting the abuse to the police, the church's leaders chose to handle the matter internally, allowing Eady to continue working in other churches and potentially exposing more victims to abuse.

- In 2009 at New Bethany Baptist Church in Jacksonville, Florida, allegations of sexual abuse were leveled against the church's pastor, Darrell Gilyard. Church leaders were accused of covering up the abuse and allowing Gilyard to remain in a position of authority despite previous allegations of sexual misconduct.

- In 2018 Andy Savage, a "teaching pastor," resigned from Highpoint Church in Memphis, Tennessee, after admitting to a "sexual incident" with a 17-year-old female congregant ten years earlier. The revelation came to light when the victim shared her story in a blog post.

- Also in 2018 Frank Page, who served as the president and CEO of the Southern Baptist Convention's Executive Committee, resigned after admitting to a "morally inappropriate relationship." While the specific details of the relationship were not disclosed, his resignation highlighted concerns about how such cases were handled within the SBC.

- In 2019 an investigation by *The Washington Post* revealed that at least 35 Southern Baptist pastors and church officials were convicted or pleaded guilty to sex crimes involving minors since 1998. In one instance, at Frederick Boulevard Baptist Church in St. Joseph, Missouri, the church leaders failed to report sexual abuse allegations to authorities and instead quietly dismissed the offending pastor.

- In 2020 Bryan Loritts, a prominent pastor and author, faced controversy when it became known that he failed to report his brother-in-law, a youth pastor at a church where Loritts was serving as an elder, for alleged sexual misconduct with a minor. The incident raised questions about the church's handling of the situation and the lack of proper reporting.

And then there's the case of Paige Patterson, which deserves separate scrutiny. Patterson served as president of Southeastern Baptist Theological Seminary from 1992 to 2003 and of Southwestern Baptist Theological Seminary from 2003 to 2018. He was known for his traditional views on gender roles. Patterson advocated for male leadership within the church and for restricting women's roles to subordinate positions.

In 2018 Paige Patterson's pronouncements concerning women's wifely roles and tolerance of domestic abuse brought scorn upon himself and the SBC. An audio recording from 2000 resurfaced, in which Patterson spoke about a woman he had counseled who was being physically abused by her husband. In the recording, he advised her to pray for her husband and to submit to the abuse in the hope of improving the marriage. Even within the SBC, this didn't go over well. The board of trustees at Southwestern Baptist Theological Seminary voted to terminate Patterson from his position as president. This scandal stimulated much debate within the denomination about gender roles, but many continued to support Patterson and his point of view.

Dipsh*tocracy

When dipsh*ts are in charge, perhaps we should refer to such institutions as *dipsh*tocracies* instead of bureaucracies. My proposed term characterizes groups with an officious, top-down management style combined with mind-blowing incompetence or irresponsibility. To the cases in this chapter, we could add such loathsome examples as Theranos, the fraudulent blood-testing company, under the mis-leadership of Elizabeth Holmes; Silicon Valley Bank which collapsed in large part because of management's failure to diversify its lending outside the tech sector and of poor risk management generally; Donald Trump's appointment of people to top government posts for which they were grossly unqualified (e.g., Ben Carson, a surgeon, as Secretary of Housing and Urban Development; Rex Tillerson, an engineer and energy executive, as Secretary of State); and Joe Biden's remarkably inept draw-down of forces from Afghanistan, resulting in a deadly and chaotic evacuation reminiscent of America's last days in Vietnam.

Organizational culture theory, advanced by Edgar Schein, a professor at MIT Sloan School of Management, examines the shared values, beliefs, and norms that guide the behavior of people in an organization. Schein proposed that the culture within a government agency, company, or institution manifests three distinct features: *artifacts*, consisting of the physical environment, dress code, and unique jargon, for example; *espoused beliefs and values*, which are the principles and purpose the organization professes to uphold; and *basic underlying assumptions*, representing the unconscious or unspoken beliefs and practices that guide the organization's behavior.

It's not uncommon to witness a group's basic underlying assumptions conflicting with its espoused values and beliefs. For example, the cover-up of priests' sexual abuse of children by the Catholic Church contradicts everything they supposedly stand for. Similarly, the American Red Cross's mission is disaster relief (and blood drives) but their actions have repeatedly raised questions about whether they are better at amassing money than aiding people is distress.

The way that power is distributed and used within an organization can help it function productively and efficiently or can set it on a course for dipsh*tocracy. Psychologists John R. P. French and Bertram Raven introduced *power dynamics theory* in 1959. They maintained that five kinds of power can determine the performance of organizations by influencing the behavior of those within it:

- *Legitimate power* is delegated to an individual when the organization places him or her in a position of authority. For example, the general manager of a factory has legitimate power over the people working there.

- *Reward power* is the authority to give or withhold benefits, such as raises, promotions, or commendations.
- *Coercive power* derives from someone's ability to punish, terminate, or give a poor performance review.
- *Expert power* resides within a person by virtue of knowledge or skill, such as the expertise of a pilot employed by an airline.
- *Referent power* accrues to a person because of his or her charisma, personality traits, or likeability. Politicians and celebrities leverage their referent power to attract followers and further their careers.

These variations of power can be mixed and matched for either beneficial or detrimental purposes. Perhaps you've encountered the type of boss who uses reward power to grant special treatment to his or her favorite employees while leveraging coercive power to deal cruelly with other staff. It's not unusual for such people also to exploit referent power to curry favor with higher-ups. Many toxic workplaces are the byproduct of a malignant organizational culture infused with abusive power dynamics.

Even organizations that treat their personnel fairly can lapse into dipsh*tocacy, however. *Organizational learning and inertia theory* explains how this can happen. Just as every company and institution has its own internal culture, each also has different ways of acquiring and processing information and knowledge. This may not seem very interesting or important until you understand the second half of that theory – organizational inertia. Once certain facts, habits, and lessons are learned and internalized, bureaucracies may find it difficult to unlearn and re-learn as circumstances change. They get locked into the "we've always done it this way" mindset. This could be a factor in the American Red Cross's repeated fumbling in response to disasters.

Social scientists James G. March and Johan P. Olsen, who originated organizational learning and inertia theory, pointed to several factors that can contribute to internal stagnation. The *sunk cost fallacy* is "throwing good money after bad." Rather than admit failures, thereby cutting their losses, organizations sometimes lapse into denial. They continue investing time, money, and other resources to save a project that cannot be saved. Individuals sometimes do this too. An example would be someone who continues to invest money in a failing business venture because "I've already invested too much to quit now."

Another factor identified by March and Olsen is *structural inertia,* which simply means rules, policies, and practices that become roadblocks rather than beneficial operating parameters. I was a faculty member at a university that encouraged us to apply for grants. In fact, our performance evaluations took into consideration our prowess in securing grant money. However, the university made it almost impossible to accomplish this. Before submitting a grant proposal to a private foundation or government agency, professors were required to get eight administrators to sign a form giving their approval – *eight approvals*! I pointed out the absurdity of this repeatedly, to no avail.

What routinely happened with grant approvals is that some administrator would nitpick a minor point within the grant, thereby blocking it until revisions were made. At other times, the grant proposal would gather dust on someone's desk until he or she got around to reading it. Meanwhile, the deadline for the grant would pass and our efforts would be wasted.

I've won funding for many grants and contracts during my career, and I can tell you without fear of contradiction that whoever set up this eight-signature scheme knew nothing about winning grants. And yet I won two large grants for that university. Before revealing how I did it, I need to bring up Star Trek.

Fans of the sci-fi series will know about the *Kobayashi Maru* scenario, a training exercise for Starfleet cadets. It's an impossible, no-win conundrum. Whatever action the trainee decides to take will produce catastrophic results. Cadets don't know this, but the test's purpose isn't to reveal whether they'll make the right or wrong decision. It's a test of character: Will the cadet violate regulations to save innocent civilians, but provoke war with the Klingons by doing so? Or will the cadet obey regulations, avoid war with the Klingons, but allow imperiled civilians to die? Captain Kirk was the only cadet who ever beat the no-win scenario. He reprogrammed the computer simulation so it was possible to win. Now back to my story about grants.

I beat the eight-signature Kobayashi Maru scenario at that university. How, you ask? By reprogramming the scenario so that it was possible to win. I submitted grant proposals in secret, without telling anyone and without getting any approvals. When the money came rolling in, no one checked to see if I had gotten the eight signatures. They assumed that I had. And they were happy with the funding, so why go looking for reasons to reject it? Only by circumventing the organizational inertia at that school was I able to avoid becoming a victim of institutional dips*ttery.

* * *

"Egypt: Where the Israelites would still be if Moses had been a bureaucrat."

— Laurence J. Peter

Epilogue

As you're nearing the end of our adventures with dipsh*ts, it's worth mentioning again that your defensive tactics against these noxious pests are *avoid-evade-defend*. For example, I couldn't avoid the university's requirement that I get eight approval signatures before submitting a grant request. But I could evade that policy, which I did. If I had been caught, I would have presented a rousing defense, condemning the signature requirements as unreasonable and unrealistic. I would have noted that our jobs required that we seek grants, and yet the university was making it impossible to do so. And finally, I would challenge the university to compare my results with the lackluster results of faculty who obeyed their impossible rule. Fortunately, it didn't come to that.

I recommend that you hang onto this book. Here's why: Sooner or later, you'll encounter a person or a situation that will anger or confound you. You'll think to yourself, "I remember reading about something similar in that *Dipsh*t* book. There was a theory that explained the kind of havoc I've just encountered." You may find yourself referring back to these pages again and again.

You should now be able to apply dipsh*t analytics to annoying neighbors, impossible relatives, obnoxious customers, toxic bosses, aggravating coworkers, and vexatious strangers. Before, you may have written them off as jerks (or worse). Their behavior might have been offensive and foolish, but also stupefying. But now you'll be able to classify them by type. You'll consider not only their behavior, but situational factors, the root cause of their stupid and despicable acts, and the severity of the outcome. You'll be able to do all that with ease using dipsh*t analytics.

Never forget that each of us can be an occasional dipsh*ts from time to time. In that regard we're all sinners. But let's strive to avoid lapsing into noxious, irresponsible behavior. In closing, I'll leave you with the following case of a repugnant reprobate who failed to meet that standard.

Seth Thomas, age 39, of Seminole, Florida was arrested on a drunk and disorderly charge. This Florida Man was observed "yelling at traffic while walking in the roadway in front of traffic and refusing to stop," according to the police report. At the time of his arrest, Thomas was drinking a can of Florida Man Beer. This beverage, brewed in Tampa, is advertised as "brewed with a nearly criminal amount of hops and a moderate bitterness that just about matches Florida Man's general disposition." Thomas was previously arrested for (you guessed it) possession of open alcohol and disorderly intoxication.

Dipsh*t analytics for Seth "Florida Man, Florida Can" Thomas:

- **Behavior:** chronic
- **Situation:** benign
- **Cause:** habitual

- **Outcome:** 4 (damaging) for Thomas; 1 (annoying) for drivers he pestered; 2 (imposing) for the police, prosecutor, and court.

Wouldn't it be great if all dipsh*ts would self-identify as Thomas did by carrying or wearing an appropriately labeled item? Until then, we can live in hope…and avoid-evade-defend.

* * *

"Stupidity is a more dangerous enemy of the good than malice. One may protest against evil; it can be exposed and, if need be, prevented by use of force. Evil always carries within itself the germ of its own subversion in that it leaves behind in human beings at least a sense of unease. Against stupidity we are defenseless."

– Dietrich Bonhoeffer

Acknowledgements

To my editor, Patrick Whittle, I am grateful for his invaluable advice and insights during the drafting of this manuscript and for his vision in recognizing the value in a book about dipsh*ts.

To the dipsh*ts I have known, I give credit for providing the dull whetstone of stupidity against which I have sharpened the blades of my wit, knowledge, and experience. Without you, this book would not have been ~~possible~~ necessary.

Dale Hartley is a psychologist, retired university professor and dean, and is a frequent contributor to Psychology Today. He became a psychologist and professor after the Great Recession of 2008 ended his company. He is the former CEO of Lionhart Group, Ltd., which delivered education and counseling services at U.S. military bases in 14 states and Puerto Rico. Dr. Hartley loves all dogs, especially bulldogs and underdogs. He lives in New Mexico.

Find Dale online:
www.Dipsh-ts.com
Facebook: Dale Hartley
Twitter: @DaleHartleyPhD
LinkedIn: Dale Hartley PhD